I Want to Teach my CHiLD About Fitness

BY

SHAWN MCMULLEN

I Want to Teach My Child About Fitness

Produced by Susan Lingo Books™
Cover and interior by Diana Walters

12 11 10 09 08 07 06 05 9 8 7 6 5 4 3 2 1
0-7847-1764-8

Contents

Introduction

Why teach your child about fitness?

In an early scene of the classic Disney film *Mary Poppins,* the magical nanny produces a special measuring tape to show how her new wards, Jane and Michael Banks, "measure up." When asked to measure herself, Mary obliges and proudly reports the verdict. "As I expected," she reads, "Mary Poppins—practically perfect in every way."

Disney magic aside, that's really what we want for our kids, isn't it? Or at least something close. We want them to be well-rounded: emotionally stable kids who keep their feet on the ground through life's ups and downs; spiritual kids who know God and stay connected to the church; intelligent kids who do well in school and think for themselves; strong kids who are full of energy and enjoy life. In short, we want to help our kids become "practically perfect in every way."

Jesus knew what it took to live a well-rounded life. When asked which of God's commandments is the greatest, He responded, "Love the Lord your God with all your heart and with all your soul and with all your mind and with all your strength" (Mark 12:30). And He lived like that—perfectly. Of course, we can't expect our kids to live perfectly, as Jesus did, but we can give them the tools they need to become fit in the four specific areas He mentioned—heart, soul, mind, and strength. Let's see how it's done.

Shawn McMullen

Where Do You Stand?

Working toward helping your child learn about fitness and how it affects his life is an important part of parenting. The following questionnaire will help you evaluate your own strengths and weaknesses and where your own values and philosophies fit in. Circle the box with the number that best corresponds to your answer. Then add up the total of your answers and check out the How You Scored box! (Retake the quiz after reading the book to see if your score changed!)

OPTIONS

❶ **Strongly agree**
❷ **Agree somewhat**
❸ **Disagree somewhat**
❹ **Strongly disagree**

I SEE MANY BENEFITS TO BEING FIT AND HEALTHY BOTH FOR TODAY AND TOMORROW.

❶ ❷ ❸ ❹

I SET ASIDE TIME TO WORK OUT SO I KEEP UP MY STAMINA AND ENERGY.

❶ ❷ ❸ ❹

I REALIZE FITNESS IS PHYSICAL, INTELLECTUAL, EMOTIONAL, *AND* SPIRITUAL.

❶ ❷ ❸ ❹

I FIND TIMES AND WAYS TO DISCUSS THE BENEFITS OF BEING HEALTHY WITH MY CHILD.

❶ ❷ ❸ ❹

OUR FAMILY ENJOYS REGULAR TIMES OF BEING ACTIVE AND FIT TOGETHER.

❶ ❷ ❸ ❹

I ENJOY TRYING NEW THINGS AND CHALLENGING MYSELF TO BE MORE CREATIVE.

❶ ❷ ❸ ❹

I BELIEVE PERSONAL CLEANLINESS IS IMPORTANT AND AFFECTS MY OVERALL HEALTH.

❶ ❷ ❸ ❹

I KNOW HOW TO CONTROL MY ANGER AND USUALLY TALK CALMLY INSTEAD OF VENTING.

❶ ❷ ❸ ❹

I THINK THAT BEING FIT IN ALL WAYS HELPS ME SERVE GOD MORE FULLY.

❶ ❷ ❸ ❹

I BELIEVE THAT MY BODY IS GOD'S TEMPLE AND IS TO BE TAKEN CARE OF.

❶ ❷ ❸ ❹

HOW YOU SCORED

10—15 Give yourself a pat on the back! You seem to have a very healthy concept of what it means to be healthy and fit in more than just your body. The health habits you've worked so hard to adopt are the ones you want to instill in your child and will serve him well throughout his life!

16—30 Your health and fitness routines may need a little polishing. You know you should work out, eat right, and read your Bible more regularly—and you wish you could stick with your plan! Try setting a few goals in the right direction and encourage your child to work toward those same goals.

31—40 Health and fitness may be on the run more than your jogging schedule! You probably don't realize how fitness is related to serving God or others. With a few goals, some hard work, and a bit of will power, you'll be back on the path to a healthy lifestyle—and your child will have a great role model!

With All Your Heart

Loving God with all your heart is the key to emotional fitness. A meaningful relationship with God provides the emotional stability families need to control anger, weather disappointments, work through anxieties, and maintain hope.

Love provides emotional stability.

Think of a Christian family you admire. What have you noticed about the way members of this family relate to one another? Do you suppose they act differently when people aren't around? Probably not. Families like this often relate to one another privately the same way they do publicly. How do they do it? One key factor is their love for one another.

We love out of God's love for us.

Where does love come from? What is it? Why love at all? The answer to these questions is God. He is love's source, definition, and reason (1 John 4:7, 16, 19). It only seems natural that, if we want to raise loving kids in a loving environment, we should look to God as our model. When families love one another like God loves, they can weather any storm together.

If God's love is the model for family love, we need to understand certain things about it. First, God's love is free. He gives us love we can't earn. He loves us simply because He has chosen to. A child who knows she is loved is on her way to becoming a strong and stable adult.

TIPS FOR TODDLERS

Get a copy of Robert Munsch's book *Love You Forever* (Firefly Books, 1986) and read it often to your small child. The book's message will speak volumes to your child about the love parents and children share.

Convey your love to your child when you pray together. Thank God for your child and for what she means to you. Then tell God how much you want to be a good parent. You should have no trouble offering this prayer sincerely!

God's love is selfless. Think about the cross. Think about how God give up His only Son to save the world—the ultimate sacrifice. Now let's bring that concept of selfless love into our family life. Selfless love means putting your family's needs above your own. You want what's best for them, even if it costs you something. Emotionally healthy kids know their parents love them selflessly.

Think of a Christian family you admire. Jot down ways they show God's love to one another and ask your kids to do the same. Then pool your lists to create a master list of loving traits your family would like to develop. Explore what God's Word teaches about God's love and the love of Jesus Christ. And don't forget to put what you learn into practice!

Romans 12:9, 10 says, "Love must be sincere. Hate what is evil; cling to what is good. Be devoted to one another in brotherly love. Honor one another above yourselves." Read these verses with your child and talk about the four elements of love: sincerity, goodness, devotion, and honor.

Love protects, trusts, and never fails.

T*hink of love as your family's guardian: It always protects.* We express love to our kids by protecting them physically and emotionally. We shelter their fragile egos. We give them reasons to feel good about themselves. We nurture their self-esteem. Christian parents protect their kids spiritually as well. We protect our kids intellectually by encouraging their curiosity, answering honestly, and challenging them to think on their own.

T*hink of love as your family's companion: It always trusts.* Just as good friends trust each other, a loving family fosters trust among its members. Sometimes the trust factor gets put to the test, and we go out on a limb to trust our children. Sometimes they do the same for us. When families know they have each other's trust, they create a bond that's not easily broken.

Pop some popcorn and watch an episode of the TV series *Seventh Heaven* with your child. Watch for positive examples of family love. Discuss how the love of this fictional family speaks to your family's love.

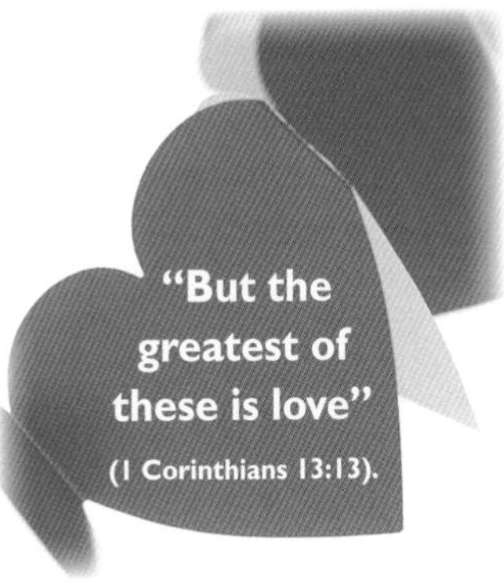

It's been said that the best thing a father can do for his kids is to love their mother. That works both ways, of course, so don't underestimate the value of your relationship. Kids need to see their parents showing affection to one another. Few things contribute as strongly to a child's sense of security.

Think of love as your family's champion: It never fails. Children feel the pain of relationship failures early. Some of their friends will lie to them, take sides against them, and desert them. Show your kids that you'll always be there for them. You'll fail, too, but make sure that when you do, you go to them immediately to admit your failure and ask forgiveness. Few things demonstrate your love more clearly.

Dedicate a family devotion time to study 1 Corinthians 13:4-8. Make it simple but meaningful. Give your kids opportunities to ask questions. Above all, lead by example. Keep a list of love's qualities beside your dresser, mirror, or night stand. Take a look at the list each evening and ask yourself which qualities you have shown your kids that day.

Love is …

Kind
Patient True
Protective Trusting
Hopeful
Persevering

Love is not …

Easily angered Proud
Boastful Failing
Rude
Keeping track of wrongdoing
Delighted by evil
Envious

Channel anger in positive ways.

When was the last time you got really angry with your spouse or one of your kids? If you could go back, would you change your response? Anger occurs even in loving families. It's not a question of *if* anger should occur but rather how we handle it *when* it occurs.

Expressing anger needs limits.

Anger is like a river. When it flows within its banks it is beneficial; when it flows beyond its banks it can be destructive. If you grew up in a home where angry outbursts were common, you may need to think about ways to channel your own anger as you teach your kids to channel theirs.

Some people justify their angry outbursts. "I just can't help it. That's how I'm wired!" Don't believe it. If you were having a boisterous argument when the phone rang, would you be able to control yourself enough to answer with a polite hello? Doesn't it seem reasonable that if we can control our anger during a phone call, we can control it during an argument?

TIPS FOR TODDLERS

As Deputy Barney Fife used to say, "Nip it! Nip it in the bud!" Some parents mistakenly think a toddler's angry outbursts are cute. But if they go unchecked, they can lead to worse behavior. When your toddler feels angry, remain calm and speak gently to him.

"Silence is one of the hardest arguments to refute."
—Josh Billings

Anger can be expressed in more ways than words. Some of us show anger by pouting and sulking. Others give the silent treatment. Some don't respond outwardly but seethe inwardly or do things behind the scenes to undermine the person with whom they're angry. None of these responses is helpful, so let's think about some positive ways to channel anger.

COFFEE BREAK

Do you ever model anger your child may be tempted to mimic?

- *Do you shout or snap at others?*
- *Do you slam doors or rattle the cookware?*
- *Do you sulk or refuse to speak?*

Watch yourself closely. Your kids certainly are!

HOW IS ANGER EXPRESSED?

- 39% SAY THEY HOLD IT IN OR HIDE IT.
- 23% OPENLY EXPRESS THEIR ANGER.
- 23% SAY THEY WALK AWAY.
- 23% CONFESS TO HAVING HIT SOMEONE.
- 17% ADMIT THEY'VE DESTROYED SOMEONE'S PROPERTY.

(CounselCare Connection, 2002)

Empower your kids. Let them know they have options when they feel angry. They can choose not to bring their anger home or not vent their anger on family members. The sooner they learn to *isolate* and *insulate*, the better. Teach your kids the "We're on the same side" principle and not have a "me against you" attitude. Hold a family meeting to talk about handling anger before it arises.

Don't let the sun set on angry feelings.

Have you ever pried the tab off the top of a soft-drink can, only to have the contents explode in your face? If you have, you understand the danger of keeping anger bottled up inside—at some point, it comes out in an explosive volley! God understands that we become angry at times, but He cautions us not to sin and to resolve conflicts quickly.

One way to control anger is to verbalize it. Talking about what makes us angry is therapeutic, even if the problem isn't quickly resolved. Communicate with nonaccusatory phrases like "I feel" and "It seems to me," instead of "You never" or "You always." These automatically put people on the defensive. Become an active listener. If we want others to listen when we're angry, we must let them express their anger as well.

"It takes one person to forgive, it takes two people to be reunited."
—Lewis B. Smedes

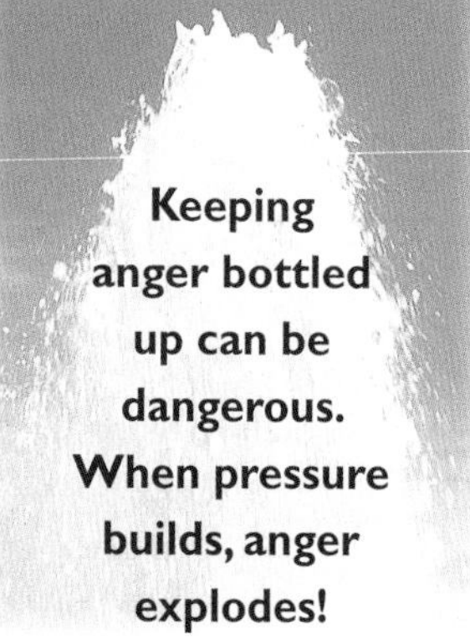

Read John 2:13-17 with your child, then ask these questions:

- *Was Jesus angry in this story?*
- *Was it okay for Him to be angry?*
- *What made Him angry?*
- *Is it okay for us to get angry sometimes?*
- *When might we become angry?*

WORDS AND PHRASES THAT ARE NONACCUSATORY.

INSTEAD OF SAYING ...	SAY THIS ...
You never respect me...	*When you say that, I feel like you don't respect me.*
You never clean up your room...	*It seems to me that your room is messy most of the time.*
You always disobey me...	*It seems like you don't pay attention when I tell you to do something.*
You always interrupt me...	*Often I feel like I can't finish a sentence when we're talking.*

Forgiveness is a powerful deterrent to anger. The Bible says, "Forgive as the Lord forgave you" (Colossians 3:13). Children are exposed to plenty of revenge and hatred in the media. Show them how to forgive. Forgive quickly. Don't use someone's failure for leverage or hold the offense over his head. When you are in the wrong, admit it. Never hesitate to say: "I was wrong." "I'm sorry." "Please forgive me."

Of course, outside your home it won't be so easy. Let your kids know that sometimes anger won't be resolved with discussions and that some people won't feel sorry. Encourage them to discover ways to refocus their anger and release it. And teach your kids not to give up, even when people don't respond at first. The best way to be rid of enemies is to make them one's friends.

Handle disappointments in productive ways.

Have you ever considered that some disappointment in your child's life can be beneficial? The truth is that some disappointment is good and healthy for children. Let's not shield our kids from all disappointment; let's find ways to walk them through it and help them learn from it.

Power struggles make everyone a loser.

A mother and father assigned chores one Saturday. The kids didn't like the tasks and complained, "We don't want to do these jobs. We didn't even get to vote on it!" The parents calmly responded, "In this home, you do not live in a democracy. You live under a benevolent dictatorship, and what we say, goes!" Parents must never abuse their authority, but they must—for everyone's sake—exercise it.

PARENTS POINTER

Some parents try hard to be a friend rather than a parent to their child. Don't make this mistake. You can be close to your child without being your child's peer.

Children test their boundaries in order to define them. They want to know where their autonomy ends and the parent's authority begins. Your resolve will be tested in many ways—tantrums, arguing, and sulking are a few techniques employed in this power struggle. And this is precisely where you must show that you're in charge.

Love your child even in the midst of power struggles!

The earlier parents establish their authority, the better. Create an atmosphere of mutual respect, starting with the way you treat and speak to your kids. Show them respect and expect the same in return. Give them the latitude you can, but draw a clear line when it's needed. It may not seem pleasant or easy, but it's our responsibility. After all, we're the adults.

Mutual respect is a powerful deterrent to power struggles. In addition to showing respect to your kids, make it a point to always show respect to your spouse in front of your kids.

Some kids "act out" to see to what degree the parent is in charge. This is a battle parents cannot afford to lose. Remember: You are the authority!

TARGET MOMENT

Power struggles can be unpleasant, but they provide opportunities to convey your love. Choose your words carefully. Don't say anything you may later regret. Let your child know that you still love her.

Recognize the difference between authority and authoritarianism. Exercise authority with humility and as a servant to your family. Don't wield power for power's sake. Don't expect your child to read your mind. If you expect a certain behavior, tell him clearly. Finally, never give the impression that you will withdraw your affection if your child displeases you.

There's no great loss without some small gain.

What do children learn from disappointments? They learn the value of delayed gratification. Sometimes things don't come to them right away. Kids may have to wait or work to obtain them. They learn patience, sympathy, and the role of disappointment in spiritual development. A. W. Tozer said, "It is doubtful that God can use any man greatly until he has hurt him deeply." What can your child learn through disappointment?

Rescuing children from disappointments often has a negative effect: many carry that mindset into adolescence, expecting others to bail them out of their problems.

When your child faces disappointment, help her see the "big picture" by keeping disappointment in perspective. Distinguish between things that are genuinely tragic and those that aren't so important. Keep in mind that kids will be kids. What may seem small to you may seem devastating to a child. Discuss what you've learned from your own disappointments and how they helped you grow.

Looking at God's big-picture plan helps kids deal with disappointment.

Encourage your child to create a learning list to evaluate disappointing circumstances. Write key questions on index cards like: *What went wrong? What has God taught me? What will I do differently?* Store the cards in a safe place and get them out when facing disappointments.

You've seen colorful woven rugs and admired their beauty, yet when you look at the underside, you see a jumbled mess of thread. Explain that our lives are like a rug God is lovingly weaving. On earth, we look up and see only the underside of the rug—a jumbled mess of circumstances. But from Heaven, God looks down on the beauty He is weaving through each of our experiences.

Create a "God is in control" reminder with your child. It can be a clay sculpture, a poster, a wooden craft, or any other item she can keep in her room to remind her that God is in control. Encourage her to display the reminder in a prominent place.

Help your child see his disappointment in light of Scripture. We should never use Scripture to dismiss a child's feelings or create unnecessary guilt, but we can and should recognize the power of Scripture to help and comfort. Hebrews 12:11 may be helpful to your child. Perhaps you'll find an opportunity to share this verse with your disappointed child and ask, "What do you think God might be teaching you through this?" "How is God showing His love to you through this?" Gently and sympathetically guide your child through this thought process. Help her understand that God is in control even when issues remain unresolved.

Read 2 Corinthians 4:16-18 and ask your child to define "light and momentary troubles." Now read 2 Corinthians 11:24-29. Ask, "How could Paul call such troubles 'light and momentary'?" Talk about perspective and hope.

Soothe anxiety in assuring ways.

A young boy frightened by a storm told his father, "I know Jesus is with me, but tonight I need someone with skin on!" God is our ultimate source of security, but until children can grasp this truth, *we* must represent God's peace and security to them.

Realize that Jesus is always with us.

When children are frightened, they often look to their parents before choosing a response of their own. One of the best ways to soothe kids' anxieties is to accept Jesus' promise: "I am with you always" (Matthew 28:20). Whether children suffer from separation anxiety, the fear of being alone, or mistrust of others, parents can use these opportunities to remind their children that Jesus is always with them.

But how can you convince a young child that a God he cannot see is constantly with him? Use the wind as an analogy. Explain that we can't see the wind, but we see what it does. Jesus is like the wind. We can't see Him, but we see what He does. He gives us strength to get through sad times and a reason to look forward to tomorrow. No, we can't see Jesus, but He's with us all the time.

No matter what is causing your child's anxiety, respect it. Take it seriously. Be sympathetic. Remember what it was like to be young and fearful. At the same time, let your child see your confidence. Remind her again that Jesus will never leave her and that God has prepared a solution to her problem, even though she can't see it at the moment.

Anticipate common causes of anxiety and talk about them before they occur.

Do you *really* remember what it was like to be young and fearful? Think of an unrealistic fear you had as a child and the accompanying emotions. Keep this in mind the next time you talk with your child about a fear he has.

Purchase a small picture of Jesus (perhaps blessing the children or as a shepherd) and hang it on your child's wall. Point your child to the picture as a visual reminder of Jesus' presence.

Select and memorize a few short Scripture verses to draw on in times of anxiety. Consider passages like Psalm 23 ("The LORD is my shepherd") and John 14:27 ("My peace I give you"). Take your child to a Christian bookstore and select a children's book or video dealing with fears. Assure him that fear and anxiety are natural and he needn't be embarrassed about things that concern him.

PSALM 23
"The LORD is my shepherd, I shall not be in want. He makes me lie down in green pastures, he leads me beside quiet waters, he restores my soul. ..."

Remember that Jesus helps us do all things.

H*is strength, not ours.* Often children demand too much of themselves. Teach them to depend on God to help when they're unable to help themselves. Paul wrote, "I can do everything through [Christ] who gives me strength" (Philippians 4:13). Remind your kids that Jesus will help them overcome their fears. It's been said, "Courage is fear that has said its prayers." Encourage your kids to go to Jesus in prayer when they feel anxious.

"Cast all your anxiety on him because he cares for you."
(1 Peter 5:7)

H*is peace, not ours.* "For he himself is our peace" (Ephesians 2:14). What a wonderful thought! Jesus Christ not only gives peace, but He has become peace for us. He is our peace. When He lives in us, we share His peace. When His Holy Spirit abides in us, He produces peace in us (Galatians 5:22). We've all gone through times when we felt we had no peace of our own. And when peace came, we knew it came from Christ, not us. Can you think of a time in your life when you desperately needed peace and Jesus gave it you? Share that experience with your child the next time she wrestles with anxiety.

"Worry is the interest paid on a problem before it occurs."
—Anne Hemphill

H*is worries, not ours.* "Cast all your anxiety on him because he cares for you" (1 Peter 5:7). Have you ever been worried and someone sensed your anxiety and said, "Relax. If any worrying needs to be done, I'll do it for you"? If you really trusted that person, you may have found those words comforting—just to know that someone else was taking up your worries. If we've ever trusted another person with our worries, we certainly ought to be able to trust God with our worries. After all, He cares for us and promises to take our worries upon himself—and He's all-powerful!

Read Philippians 4:6, 7 with your child, then ask:

- *What does God say about our anxieties?*
- *What does He promise to those who present their requests to Him?*
- *What's one worry you can give to God today?*

TIPS FOR 'TWEENS

Encourage your child to be an ambassador for Christ among her friends. Many will be worried about many things. Challenge your child to reach out with the same "do-not-worry" principles you've discussed together.

At some point kids leave behind their childlike trust and are not easily comforted. This is a critical time for parents, a time to hold to the principles we taught them as young children, but also to help them develop defenses against anxiety that respect their budding maturity, intellect, and social awareness. Stay available to your child—to listen, to pray, and to counsel when asked.

Worries grow up as kids grow up! Offer help, advice, and more empathy to your 'tween.

Celebrate hope each day!

Scan the newspaper headlines or watch the opening segment of a TV news broadcast and you're quickly reminded that we live in a troubled world. It seems as if we're surrounded by bad news, pessimism, and despair. How can we protect our kids from the kind of negative thinking that often stems from such exposure? We can help them celebrate hope each day.

God has a plan for everyone.

Hope has a profound effect on emotional stability. We like to think that children are naturally hopeful, and that may be true. But it's also true that many kids today struggle desperately—and often unsuccessfully—to find hope and meaning. How can we give our kids hope? We can remind them that God is in control, loves them, and has a plan for them.

Look for God's plans, and you'll find hope!

Suicide is the #3 cause of death among Americans ages 10–24. (National Institute of Mental Health, 2003)

God is a God of hope. Jeremiah 29:11 tells us that God has "plans to give you hope and a future." Tell your child that God has a plan for her. It's a plan for prosperity and hope. It's a plan for the future—something to look forward to. Once kids know God has a plan for them, they can begin the adventure of discovering that plan!

Explain to your child that God has given us many principles for Christian living in His Word. We can discover His will about issues such as forgiveness, humility, purity, and love by reading the Bible. Psalm 37:4 says: "Delight yourself in the LORD and he will give you the desires of your heart." What a thought!

TARGET MOMENT

Tragedies often provide teachable moments. If your newspaper runs a story of a youth suicide, take that opportunity to pray with your child for the family of the victim. Talk about the hope we have in Christ and the plan God has for each of us.

Circumstances, counselors, and our own hearts help us understand God's plan, but make sure your child knows the Bible is the true authority in this area. Share the questions below with your child and encourage her to use them when making decisions.

Share these questions with your child to use when making decisions and seeking God's plans.

(1) *Is it beneficial?—"Not everything is beneficial" (1 Corinthians 6:12).*

(2) *Does it bring me under its power?—"I will not be mastered by anything" (1 Corinthians 6:12).*

(3) *Does it hurt others?—"I will not cause him to fall" (1 Corinthians 8:13).*

(4) *Does it glorify God?—"Do it all for the glory of God" (1 Corinthians 10:31)*

God is already in tomorrow.

We may not know what tomorrow will bring, but we can know God will be there when it comes. Think about it like this. If you could select anyone to be in charge of your tomorrows, wouldn't you choose someone who has the authority and power to do something about them, someone who always has your best interests at heart? That decision is not ours to make, but thankfully, it has already been made for us. God *is* in charge of our tomorrows.

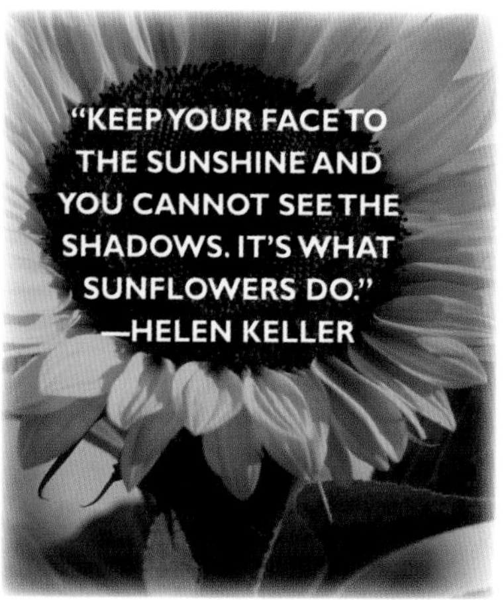

Read 1 Samuel 7:7-12. The stone Samuel named "Ebenezer" was a reminder to Israel that God had helped them, an object they could look to whenever they felt uncertain about their future. What can your family use as an "Ebenezer stone," a reminder that God will always help you?

BUILDING HOPE

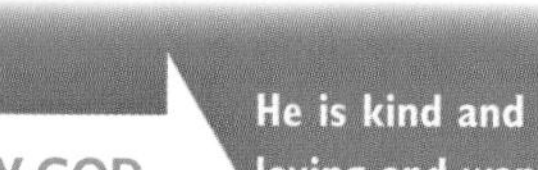

Knowing God is in tomorrow gives us hope. And hope is like light at the end of a tunnel. Job had this kind of hope. Even when it seemed everything in his life had gone wrong, Job hoped against hope. He couldn't begin to understand what God was permitting, yet he knew God was in control and in tomorrow. That gave him hope to persevere in his trials.

key point
HOPE LEADS TO PERSEVER-ANCE.

key point
GOD IS OUR SECURITY.

Is there a secret to this hope? No, there is no secret, no magic formula, but there is a process we can follow. First, *know God*. The more we know God, the more we place our confidence in Him. *Trust God*. You can know He'll always do the right thing. Then *rest in God*. If you believe He's taking care of your problems and tomorrows, you're less inclined to worry about them yourself.

God is the only true source of emotional strength and security, so talk to your child in ways that underscore this fact, ways that express your own hope. Try this exercise when your child seems anxious about the future. Think back with your child to an anxious time. Invite your child to tell you how she felt then. Ask, "What do you think God was doing at that time?" Help your child see the good God brought. Conclude by observing, "If God did that for us then, why wouldn't He do the same this time?" End with a prayer expressing your hope and asking for God's continued help and encouragement.

Remind your child that God is the true source of strength, security, and hope—and this brings us joy!

TIPS FOR 'TWEENS

Sometimes kids need reminders that God is in control. If your 'tween is anxious about the future, slip a note into his lunch with a Scripture verse or a few words from you that say, "Don't despair. God is in charge."

With All Your Soul

Loving God with all your soul is the key to spiritual fitness. We become spiritually fit as we grow closer to God and to His Son Jesus Christ through our study of the Bible, our dependence on God's Holy Spirit, and prayer.

We grow spiritually as we grow closer to God.

If you've ever kept houseplants, you've probably noticed they grow toward the light. In its own way, a plant recognizes—and grows toward—its source of nourishment and strength. Growing Christians recognize God as their source of nourishment and strength and become spiritually fit as they grow closer to Him.

Trust in and rely on God.

Strength-training experts tell us the more we exercise, the stronger our muscles become. But did you realize the process involves the *tearing down* of muscle fiber? Weight lifting actually tears down muscle fiber so it comes back stronger when it is rebuilt. We operate by a similar principle in our spiritual lives. Sometimes we must do difficult things—straining and stretching our faith—in order to grow spiritually. Trusting God and relying on Him are keys to spiritual development.

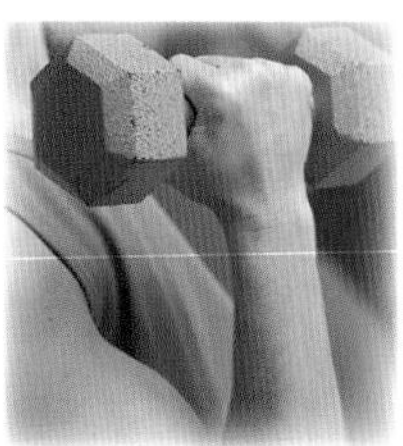

Exercising our faith is like exercising our muscles—it just becomes stronger over time!

Most of us are acquainted with many people but trust only a few. The people we trust have earned our confidence. It begins when we place our trust in someone and give that person opportunities to prove worthy of our trust. The more trustworthy the person proves to be, the more trusting we become. This is how we want our kids to relate to God.

Kids learn to trust (or mistrust) early.

Talk to your children about times in your life when you trusted God and relied on Him. Tell them what happened and how you saw God at work in your circumstances. In addition, read the biographies of faithful Christians like Hudson Taylor and George Muller with your kids. Their testimonies have inspired generations of Christians to greater faith and trust in God.

Let your kids fall backwards onto their beds. Then have them try it again with their eyes closed. Ask:

- *Were you afraid? Why or why not?*
- *How did you know you weren't going to fall?*
- *In what ways did you trust the bed to protect you?*
- *In what ways is this like trusting God to catch you when you have fears or troubles?*

Obey and honor God.

Obedience is rooted in love and trust. We want our children to obey out of love, not out of fear. The same is true regarding our obedience to God. We study His Word and obey His commands, even when His commands seem to run counter to our own thoughts and desires. We obey because we love and trust God. In human relationships, the more trust we give to someone, the closer we grow. The same principle is at work in our relationship to God.

DON'T FORGET

- **Demonstrate obedience in your own life.**
- **Expect obedience from your children.**
- **Discuss the relationship between obeying and honoring God.**
- **Acknowledge obedience with approval and encouragement.**

"Obedience is the fruit of faith."
—Christina Rossetti

Another way we grow closer to God is by honoring Him in all we do. The word "honor" comes from the Latin *honos*, referring to a person's good name or public esteem. In its verb form, it means to regard or treat someone with deference and respect. We honor God in many ways—through obedience, worship, devotion, and service. When we live by the guidelines God has given us, we bring honor and glory to His name—we show that He is worthy of our obedience.

TARGET MOMENT

Think about obeying God and why it's important, then discuss the following questions:

- **What does it mean to obey God?**
- **How does obeying God tell Him we love and respect Him?**
- **What might happen if we don't obey God?**

When children are young they may obey a parent's command because the parent is visible—and because the parent has the potential to respond immediately if they disobey. Because they cannot see God, some children may believe the consequences of their disobedience to Him will be ignored or even postponed indefinitely. As Christian parents, our task is to help our children understand that God is with them and He knows everything.

PARENTS POINTER

One way to encourage your child to honor God is to use the phrase often. If your child is tempted to do something wrong, don't merely say, "No, that's wrong." Instead, say, "No, that wouldn't honor God." In the same way, when talking about something positive, say, "I think this would honor God, don't you?"

Remind children that obedience is a demonstration of love, respect, and honor.

Take advantage of teachable moments to remind your child that God is with us always, that He sees everything we do, and that we obey because we love God and want to please Him. When you pray with your child, acknowledge God's presence in your lives. In conversation, tell your child what God's constant presence means to you. And reinforce the truth that God is with us always because He loves and cares for us.

Seek God in all you do.

How do you feel when someone seeks your advice? You probably feel good because it shows the person has faith in you and your judgment. The bigger the problem, the more selective we become about the counsel we seek. This should hold true in our relationship with God. The more intimately we know Him, and the more we stand in awe of His wisdom and power, the more likely we are to seek His counsel in all matters.

"Ask and it will be given to you; seek and you will find; knock and the door will be opened to you." (Matthew 7:7)

TIPS FOR TODDLERS
Begin in infancy to pray with your child at bedtime, and you will be setting the stage for future prayer times in their toddler years and later on.

God wants to be sought. But sadly, some people view this as a last resort. Either they wait until they've exhausted all other options before seeking God, or they carefully develop their own plans, their own response, and only then ask God to bless what they've decided to do. Let's not make those mistakes. Seeking God must become our first response to every situation.

Teach your child that we seek with our hearts! "You will seek me and find me when you seek me with all your heart." (Jeremiah 29:13)

Seeking God means more than asking for His help, however. The word *seek* comes from a Greek word that describes not only seeking God's counsel but seeking God in worship. In Psalm 63:1, David says, "O God, you are my God, earnestly I seek you; my soul thirsts for you, my body longs for you." Certainly we must seek God in prayer, but we must also seek Him by dwelling constantly in His presence and living consistently in His fellowship.

- *Why is seeking God in prayer often our last resort rather than our first step?*
- *What does that say about our faith?*
- *How can that be corrected?*

When our daughters were young, I arose early to have my daily devotions. Often one of them would crawl onto my lap and sit with me as I read the Bible and prayed. In a small way, I felt I was conveying to them the importance of seeking God. There are other ways to impress this on our kids, too. When your child has a problem, listen carefully and ask, "Have you prayed?" Share prayer about the issue together.

In addition to occasionally inviting your young children to join you as you pray, how about allowing them to join you sometimes as you pray with your spouse or a friend?

We grow spiritually fit by loving Jesus.

Perhaps the best way to please God is to become like Him. Paul said, "Be imitators of God … and live a life of love, just as Christ loved us" (Ephesians 5:1, 2). There you have it. Imitate God and love as Jesus loves—two key components in our spiritual growth.

Choose to make Jesus your life's role model.

Nearly every kid has a role model. It may be a family member or friend. It may a professional athlete, a musician, or a movie star. The point is, we've all come in contact with people we'd like to model our lives after. When children are very young, they don't pick their role models—they come built into the family unit. It's vital that parents provide positive role models for their children from the beginning—so that when kids begin choosing their own role models, they will have a standard to guide them.

Ask your 'tween whom she respects and admires. Don't be critical of her choices, but take time to talk about what makes a good role model and what qualities we ought to seek in our role models.

We can give our children positive role models when we make Jesus *our* role model. We can show our kids—by example—what it means to love God and pattern our lives after Christ. Don't be afraid of failing. In fact, our failures become opportunities to demonstrate the wonder of God's grace and mercy as we acknowledge our faults and humbly seek forgiveness.

The power of parental example cannot be underestimated. In *Faith of the Fatherless* (Spence Publishing Company, 2000) author Paul Vitz suggests that the way children see their earthly fathers directly affects the way they see their heavenly Father. Vitz examined the childhoods of prominent atheists and discovered that in all instances the atheist's father was either absent or abusive. The opposite was true for prominent theists. Kids who see Christ in both their father and mother are much more likely to

TARGET MOMENT

When you have failed in your relationship with your kids, don't sweep it under the rug. Talk about it, seek your kids' forgiveness, then point them to Jesus, who never fails us.

When we make Jesus Christ our life's role model, we must clearly communicate that choice to our children. When was the last time you confided that your greatest desire is to imitate God and love like Jesus loves? Take time to communicate this vital principle to your child—and then give your words credibility by the way you live.

10 TIMES TO TALK!

- AT THE BREAKFAST TABLE
- ON THE WAY TO SCHOOL
- JUST BEFORE BEDTIME
- IN THE DENTIST'S OFFICE
- IN A TRAFFIC JAM
- AT THE FOOD COURT
- ON A WALK
- AT THE SUPPER TABLE
- WHILE WAITING IN THE CAR
- ANYTIME AT ALL!

"The question for the child is not 'Do I want to be good?' but 'Whom do I want to be like?'"
—Bruno Bettelheim

Forgive others as Jesus has forgiven us.

There is no better feeling than the experience of being forgiven. Think of a time you seriously hurt someone you love. Do you remember how terrible you felt? Did the one you offended say, "It's okay, I forgive you"? When we realize God has forgiven all our sins in Christ, we experience forgiveness in a powerful way. God's mercy washes over us and renews us. Then and only then can we follow Paul's instruction: "Forgive as the Lord forgave you" (Colossians 3:13).

"The weak can never forgive. Forgiveness is the attribute of the strong."
—Mohandas Gandhi

TIPS FOR 'TWEENS

The next time your 'tween does something that requires forgiveness, use the time to talk about how forgiveness feels. Ask:

- **How did you feel before you were forgiven?**
- **How did you feel afterward?**
- **How is forgiveness a gift of love?**

Read and discuss these Scriptures about sin and forgiveness with your child:

- *Psalm 103:12*
- *Isaiah 1:18*
- *Isaiah 44:22*
- *I John 2:12*

How much Christ has forgiven you? The more we think about it, the more apparent it becomes: God's forgiveness knows no limitations in the Christian's life. When we've carefully considered the extent of our own forgiveness in Christ, and when the forgiveness we've received becomes the standard of the forgiveness we offer, we ought to be able to forgive everyone of every offense against us—if we have learned to forgive others as the Lord has forgiven us.

Sometimes it's hard to forgive the people who've hurt us. Remember: God never asks us to do what we can't do, and we can seek God's help in a special way. If you don't think you can forgive someone, be honest with God. Say, "Lord, I can't do this on my own. I don't want to forgive. Please give me the strength to do what You've called me to do." Remember, God is faithful.

IF WE FORGIVE OTHERS, THEN WE WILL BE FORGIVEN.

When it comes to teaching our children to forgive as the Lord forgives, our own examples become our most powerful teaching tool. Practice forgiveness at home. Some parents are quick to overlook or forgive an offense at work, at church, or in the community—but let a member of their own family offend them in a similar way, and the feud may last for days or even weeks. When it comes to forgiveness, shouldn't our families get our best?

TRY THIS!

This activity for older children can be done in your home (around the fireplace) or on a camping trip (around a campfire). Talk about the way God forgives our sins. Have everyone write down several sins they struggle with. Pray, seeking God's forgiveness, then crumple the lists and throw them into the fire, representing the fact that those sins are remembered no more.

We grow spiritually through God's Word.

The Bible is a unique book, different from every other book in the world. It is inspired by God, it's active, has living power, and always accomplishes its purpose. No wonder our spiritual growth depends on our study and application of God's Word!

Study to show yourself approved.

God's Word is the key component to spiritual fitness, and there are no quick fixes or shortcuts. If we want to grow spiritually, we must spend time reading, meditating on, and applying God's Word to our lives. The apostle Paul wrote, "Do your best to present yourself to God as one approved" (2 Timothy 2:15). The phrase "do your best" might also be translated "be diligent" or "make every effort."

Plan a series of family devotional times around Psalm 119 (perhaps verses 9-16, 33-40, 89-96, 97-104, and 105-112). Use these times to talk about the benefits we derive from God's Word.

Effort often depends on our motivation. In 2 Timothy 3:16 Paul gives us several motivational factors for becoming diligent students of Scripture, including "teaching, rebuking, correcting and training in righteousness." Parents who want their children to grow up loving and obeying God will expose them to God's Word, teach them His will, and lead them to God's Word to expose wrong thinking and dangerous philosophies.

Culture and media inundate our kids with false and misleading ideas.

When we recognize behavioral problems in our kids, God's Word helps us find principles to correct the problems. Not only does God's Word correct wrong behavior; it encourages right behavior. Sooner or later our children will be on their own, making their own decisions. Our goal as parents is to give them the tools they need to make wise choices. By taking kids to the Word in their early years, we establish positive patterns of decision making that carry into adulthood.

THE BIBLE

- Power to make us holy (John 17:17)
- Living and active (Hebrews 4:12)
- Always achieves its purpose (Isaiah 55:11)
- Inspired by God (2 Timothy 3:16)

Try this simple approach to help your children develop the habit of going to God's Word. Keep a Bible (a modern translation with a concordance) in a designated place in your home as your "family Bible." When your child asks a question or faces a problem, go together to the family Bible to get the answer. The more you do this, the more likely your children will be to follow your example later.

TIPS FOR TODDLERS

Purchase a copy of *Baby's First Bible* **or** *My Good-Night Bible* **(Standard Publishing) for your toddler. Allow your toddler to carry a Bible to Sunday school to help him develop a love for God's Word at an early age.**

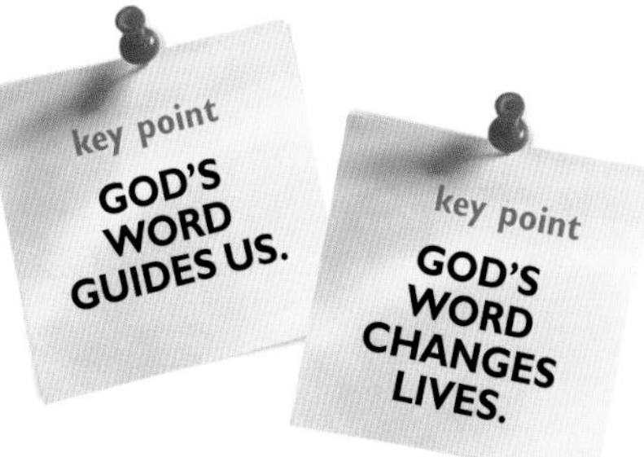

Use and apply God's Word in your life.

Following His baptism, Jesus "was led by the Spirit into the desert to be tempted by the devil" (Matthew 4:1). Satan did his best to make Jesus stumble, but each time Jesus countered the temptation with a quotation from God's Word. He knew the Scriptures, had committed them to memory, and had them at the ready when He needed them. We can learn to use and apply God's Word in our lives by following three simple steps.

key point

SPEND TIME IN GOD'S WORD.

NO AMOUNT OF STUDY OR MEMORIZATION WILL HELP IF WE'RE NOT WILLING TO LOOK INWARDLY AND APPLY GOD'S WORD TO OUR LIVES.

Read and study. The more time we spend in God's Word, the more understanding we gain. At times we need to read the Bible in a relaxed way, listening as God speaks to us through the pages of Scripture. At other times we must dig deeply into the Word in order to mine out its limitless riches. The important thing is that we carve time out of our busy schedules to do this regularly, even daily.

Help your kids create Scripture memory cards. Write down a few verses on index cards or construction paper. Choose verses your child wants to work on. Make cards for yourself, too!

M*emorize and meditate.* "I have hidden your word in my heart that I might not sin against you" (Psalm 119:11). Memorizing God's Word keeps it in our hearts and minds. Don't be intimidated by the thought of memorizing Scripture. Take a few words or phrases at a time. You'll be surprised at what you can do. Try passages that remind you God is in control (Romans 8:28) or that your duty is to raise your kids to know God (Ephesians 6:4).

E*xamine and apply.* Reading Scripture without applying it is like looking into a mirror and immediately forgetting what we look like (James 1:23, 24). One way we—and our children—can get the most out of the time we spend in God's Word is to make sure we ask questions such as the following as we read:

1. *What does the passage mean?*
2. *What does it say to me personally?*
3. *Is it pointing to something I need to change in my life? If so, what?*
4. *What is my plan for making this change?*

Use questions such as these to help your child experience the illuminating light reflected in God's Word!

TARGET MOMENT

When you think your child is not seeing himself clearly in the mirror of God's Word (James 1:23, 24), gently help him see the truth. Point out where his life or attitude is conflicting with God's Word.

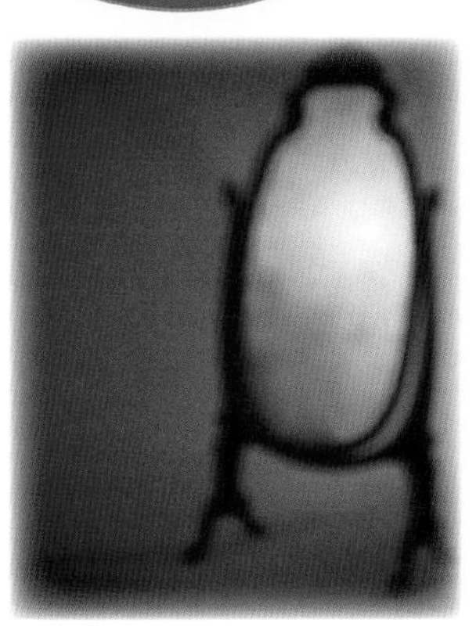

We grow spiritually fit through God's Spirit.

Near the end of His life on earth Jesus said to His disciples, "It is for your good that I am going away. Unless I go away, the Counselor will not come to you; but if I go, I will send him to you" (John 16:7). The Counselor Jesus referred to is God's Holy Spirit, given to every believer to lead and guide us in our Christian lives. What an incredible gift for us and our children!

Allow God's Spirit to work through you.

Jesus said, "I will ask the Father, and he will give you another Counselor to be with you forever—the Spirit of truth. The world cannot accept him, because it neither sees him nor knows him. But you know him, for he lives with you and will be in you" (John 14:16, 17). God's Holy Spirit lives *with* and *in* every Christian. The Holy Spirit is not an impersonal force but a living, personal, spiritual being—our Comforter, Helper, Advocate, and Counselor.

"Prayer is the spirit speaking truth to Truth."
–Philip James Bailey

TIPS FOR TODDLERS

Help your toddler understand God's Spirit as a helper. Helpers don't do all the work but aid in the work you do. That's how God's Spirit helps us—not doing all the work of living, but rather helping us do God's work.

The Holy Spirit helps us in many ways, all of which lead to our sanctification. He leads us (Romans 8:14), helps us resist temptation and sin (Romans 8:13; Galatians 5:16), produces the fruit of holiness in our lives (Galatians 5:22, 23), helps us when we pray (Romans 8:26), and helps us understand and appreciate God's love for us (Ephesians 3:16-19).

If we're to help our kids understand the Spirit's presence in their lives, we need a clear picture of how the Spirit works. Paul wrote, "But the fruit of the Spirit is love, joy, peace, patience, kindness, goodness, faithfulness, gentleness and self-control" (Galatians 5:22, 23), and Jesus said, "I am the vine; you are the branches. If a man remains in me and I in him, he will bear much fruit; apart from me you can do nothing" (John 15:5). We're to live by these principles.

The Spirit helps us understand God's love and helps us remain faithful to God and His Word.

We can use this analogy to show our children how the Holy Spirit works. Jesus is the vine and we are the branches. The work of the branch is not to produce fruit, but to *bear* fruit. Our focus is not on producing the fruit of the Spirit but simply remaining, with the Spirit's help, attached to the vine—Jesus. As we remain in Christ, God's Spirit bears fruit within our lives.

key point

THE HOLY SPIRIT LIVES WITHIN US.

Some biblical names given to the Holy Spirit:

Spirit of truth (John 14:16, 17)
Counselor (John 14:26)
Spirit of life (Romans 8:2)
Spirit of holiness (Romans 1:4)
Spirit of wisdom (Ephesians 1:17)
Eternal Spirit (Hebrews 9:14)

Serve others through God's Spirit.

Another remarkable activity of the Holy Spirit has to do with the gifts He gives us for ministry. The Holy Spirit gives gifts to believers so that we may use them for the benefit of others. Peter put it this way: "Each one should use whatever gift he has received to serve others, faithfully administering God's grace in its various forms" (1 Peter 4:10).

What are these gifts? The Bible doesn't give us an exhaustive list, but Paul lists seven categories that most spiritual gifts fall into:

- *Prophesying*—speaking to give encouragement.
- *Serving*—providing ministry to others.
- *Teaching*—presenting truth clearly.
- *Encouraging*—building others up.
- *Leadership*—motivating and directing others.
- *Contributing to others' needs*—giving generously.
- *Showing mercy*—alleviating the distress of others.

key point

WE ALL HAVE A GIFT FOR MINISTRY.

Let your kids see you using God's gifts to serve at church. Consider these areas:

- *Musical talents*
- *Teaching Sunday school*
- *Business skills*
- *Cooking for get-togethers*

The notion of discovering our spiritual gifts has frustrated many Christians. God doesn't play games by giving us gifts secretly and then leaving us to search frantically for them. Nowhere in Scripture are we commanded to discover our spiritual gifts. Still, it only makes sense that we should know our strengths and focus our energies there.

It's likely that your older child is developing an awareness of her spiritual gifts. Encourage her to use her gifts in ministry. Talk to the leaders of your church to see if there are areas you can help your child plug into.

PARENTS POINTER

Several tests have been developed to help Christians determine their gifts for ministry. Here are two to check out:

- Spiritual Gifts Inventory: Church Growth Institute, P.O. Box 4404, Lynchburg, VA 24502.
- Trenton Spiritual Gifts Analysis: Charles E. Fuller Institute, P.O. Box 91990, Pasadena, CA 91109-1990.

How can we teach our kids to serve others through God's Spirit? Make serving others a priority in your life. Another way is to plan family service projects. It may be as simple as walking next door to rake a neighbor's yard or as complicated as planning a short-term missions trip. Whatever you choose to do, credit God and His Holy Spirit with your motivation to serve others!

We grow spiritually fit through prayer.

There is great power in the Christian's prayer. Faithful prayer is the key to spiritual growth and growing closer to God on a daily basis. This is true both for Christian individuals and Christian families.

There's power in faithful prayer.

God answers prayer. Jesus promised, "You may ask me for anything in my name, and I will do it" (John 14:14). The apostle John observed, "If we ask anything according to his will, he hears us. And if we know that he hears us—whatever we ask—we know that we have what we asked of him" (1 John 5:14, 15). If we believe God, we must believe He answers prayer—in His time and in His way.

Why does nearly every prayer we hear conclude with the phrase, "in Jesus' name, amen"? It's because Jesus invited us to pray "in His name." To pray in the name of Jesus means we can approach God in prayer because Jesus made it possible, and He intercedes for us. We can "approach the throne of grace with confidence, so that we may receive mercy and find grace to help us in our time of need" (Hebrews 4:16).

TARGET MOMENT

The time you spend in prayer creates peace and contentment in daily living, and the quiet confidence you show reinforces the power of prayer to your kids.

Let your child create a prayer notebook. Make three columns on each page: prayer concerns, the date you begin praying about the concern, and the date the prayer was answered. Ask your child to show you his notebook from time to time so you can talk together about the answers he has received.

Explain to older kids that any positive number multiplied by infinity equals infinity, no matter how small the number. Explain that this principle works in prayer, too. Even the smallest "mustard seed" of faith, when placed in God's infinite hands, wields infinite power!

GOD'S POWER AND LOVE ARE INFINITE!

What can we expect when we pray? We can expect God to do what He has promised. Jesus said, "If you have faith as small as a mustard seed, you can say to this mountain, 'Move from here to there' and it will move. Nothing will be impossible for you" (Matthew 17:20). Assure your child that God has promised to hear our prayers and answer them—in His time and in His way.

key point

GOD HEARS OUR PRAYERS.

Begin nurturing a pattern of prayer in your child's life. Whether it's a simple mealtime prayer or a rambling "God-bless-everybody-I've-ever-known" bedtime prayer, children should be encouraged to pray at all times and on all occasions. The more your family prays, the more opportunities you will have to see God at work in your lives. Teach your kids by word and example to "pray continually" (1 Thessalonians 5:17).

"Prayer—secret, fervent, believing prayer—lies at the root of all personal godliness."
—William Carey

PARENTS POINTER

As you teach your kids to pray, don't force them to pray in situations if they're uncomfortable. Some kids are shy about praying aloud. Respect your child's individuality.

Prayer demonstrates humility.

Jesus was devoted to prayer. He spent the entire night in prayer before calling His disciples and spent His final hours agonizing in prayer in the garden. Jesus' devotion to prayer was coupled with humility in prayer. "During the days of Jesus' life on earth, he offered up prayers and petitions with loud cries and tears to the one who could save him from death, and he was heard because of his reverent submission" (Hebrews 5:7).

Jesus often left His disciples and went to solitary places to pray.

Jesus' example of reverent submission encourages us to pray with humility. Explain to your child that when we pray, we approach God knowing we deserve nothing from Him. Our attitude is like that of Daniel, who said, "We do not make requests of you because we are righteous, but because of your great mercy" (Daniel 9:18). No wonder Christians through the ages have regularly dropped to their knees when they prayed. What a powerful way to show humility before God!

Illustrate humility in prayer by discussing the various postures of prayer, such as praying on knees, folding hands, or closing eyes. Each is a symbol of humility before God.

We can teach our kids to pray in all situations and with confidence that God will hear and answer their requests.

Few things convict us of the power of prayer like personal experience!

Jesus' disciples asked Him, "Lord, teach us to pray" (Luke 11:1). If we want to learn to pray as Jesus prayed, we must be willing to follow His example. We can begin by following His example in our devotion to prayer and in the humility with which we pray. There's an interesting principle at work here. The greater our devotion to prayer, and the more humility with which we pray, the more confidence we have in prayer—confidence in the God we trust.

Share Luke 18:9-14 with your child as you remind him about humility in prayer. Then discuss these questions:

- *Who showed pride in this story?*
- *Who showed humility?*
- *Whose prayer was heard?*
- *How can we humbly thank God for His answers?*

How can you affirm to your child God's answers to prayers? It might be as simple as saying, "Wow, that was an answer to prayer, wasn't it?" Be sure to thank God for answering all your prayers.

For kids to grasp the great power of prayer, we need to show them answers to prayer. When you pray for specific needs as a family, do you thank God for the answer He provides? If not, you're missing a marvelous opportunity to reaffirm how God answers prayer. Here's one suggestion. Pray for safety before you leave on a family trip. When you return, ask everyone to thank God for the safety you requested. Acknowledge all of God's answers to prayer.

With All Your Mind

Loving God with all your mind is the key to intellectual fitness. God gave us minds so we could know, understand, and worship Him. We honor Him when we use our minds in constructive and creative ways.

God gave us special gifts and talents.

One child loves math class and willingly volunteers to work out problems on the chalkboard. Another lives for recess and organized sports. Still another thrives in the art room, creating masterpieces in clay and on canvas. Why are they so different? Because that's how God created us. We all have unique gifts, abilities, and interests.

"Smarts" come in many forms.

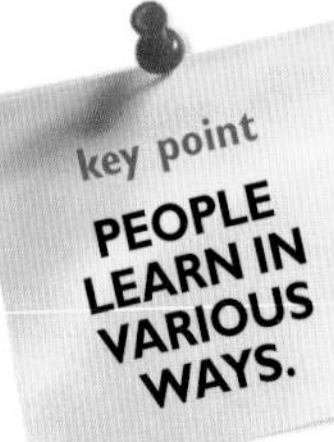

All children don't think and learn alike. Psychologist Howard Gardner, author of *Frames of Mind: The Theory of Multiple Intelligences* (Howard Gardner, 1983) identifies seven types of intelligence we might see in children:

- *Linguistic* (reading, writing, word puzzles)
- *Logical-Mathematical* (solving problems, strategy games)
- *Bodily-Kinesthetic* (bodily sensations and movement)
- *Spatial* (images, drawing, building)
- *Musical* (music, audio, rhythms)
- *Interpersonal* (effective communicators, outgoing)
- *Intrapersonal* (self-motivated, may be shy)

We think and learn differently, process information and communicate differently. We have unique strengths and weaknesses. Have you ever wondered how the same parents can raise the same children in the same household under the same conditions, yet each child seems to turn out differently from the others? Relate to your child according to his individual character, leading him on a course that fits his specific temperament.

TARGET MOMENT

Take time to read and reflect on Proverbs 22:6 with your spouse or another parent. Then consider …

- **What does "in the way he should go" mean in regard to your child?**
- **What does this verse promise?**
- **What will you do as a result?**

How does your child learn? See if you can identify one or two favored learning styles based on Gardner's seven intelligence types. Then keep this learning style in mind as you teach, correct, and guide your child.

LEFT hemisphere:	RIGHT hemisphere:
logic	intuition
mathematics	feelings
categorizing	sensitivity
rationality	daydreaming
deductive reasoning	spatial concepts
abstractions	first impressions
time sequences	visualizing
rules	creativity
	color

Wise parents will not expect the same thing from each child. They relate to each child in the way that works best for that individual. They don't compare. Their children do not hear, "Why can't you be an A-student like your brother?" or "Why aren't you interested in tennis like your sister?" Instead of forcing children into a mold, wise parents identify the unique interests of their children and encourage them to excel in those areas.

Use the gifts God has given you.

We've considered how God gifts and equips us for service. Each of us has one or more unique abilities, and God wants us to use them for His glory in service to others. The apostle Peter wrote, "Each one should use whatever gift he has received to serve others, faithfully administering God's grace in its various forms. If anyone speaks, he should do it as one speaking the very words of God. If anyone serves, he should do it with the strength God provides, so that in all things God may be praised through Jesus Christ" (1 Peter 4:10, 11). From this verse we might place the gifts God gives us into two categories: speaking gifts and serving gifts.

key point

OUR ABILITIES COME FROM GOD.

Speaking gifts might include any gift that involves communication, including public speaking, teaching, and encouraging. Serving gifts include any gift that involves the work of our hands, such as giving, leading, and showing mercy. The Bible is filled with examples of people who served God with the unique gifts God gave them. God gave Moses' brother Aaron a special ability to speak before Pharaoh. Paul used his abilities as a tentmaker, and Apollos used logic and oratory to preach the gospel.

Encourage your child to use what God has given by emphasizing that our minds and abilities are gifts that God expects us to use wisely.

GIFTS OF COMMUNICATION HELP PEOPLE ENCOURAGE ONE ANOTHER!

As we serve God, we are serving Him with our minds as well. Paul describes how our service and minds are linked together. Your child needs to understand that, whether we use gifts of speaking or gifts of serving, our hearts and minds are the most important tools we can use! Help your child realize that it's through using her heart and mind that she can understand God's will, then respond using the gifts God gives her to serve others and honor Him.

Perhaps you've seen your child display certain talents and abilities. Let your child know that you see these qualities in her life. Find ways around the house to let your child use her special talents. From there, encourage her to find ways to use her gifts in school, at church, or in your community. Don't do all the work for her, but encourage her to show initiative as she discovers ways to use her mind and talents.

WHAT TALENTS AND ABILITIES DOES YOUR CHILD POSSESS?

Instead of looking for opportunities to serve, create them! By word and example, show your child how to serve proactively.

Nurture creativity and curiosity.

Many wonderful discoveries have resulted from someone's creativity and curiosity. Who knows what might happen in the years to come if we nurture creativity and curiosity in our kids today?

Don't be afraid to try new things.

The comedian Grady Nutt told the story of a man who bought a new radio, tuned it to his favorite station, and removed all its knobs. He had tuned it to the one thing he wanted to hear, and he had no desire to hear anything new or different. We all fall into ruts from time to time. Parents who want to nurture creativity and curiosity in their children will take pains to avoid ruts and will encourage their children to do the same.

Trying new things stretches, sharpens, and improves our minds. Scientists have discovered that our brains continually rewire and adapt even into old age and that mental exercises like reading, writing, and working puzzles may reduce the risks of Alzheimer's disease in some people. Older adults aren't the only ones who benefit from having active minds. That's why encouraging kids to use their minds and try new things helps during school years—and aids them throughout their lives.

TRY THIS!

Do you want your kids to try new things? Then try new things with them! Learn a new hobby. Try a new recipe. Craft a family motto. Write a song together—and have fun!

Some children don't like to try new things—hobbies, sports, and other pursuits—because they fear failure. They're afraid they won't be good enough or competitive enough in certain activities, so they don't attempt them. Remind your child that no one is perfect and he doesn't have to excel in everything he does. Encourage your child to try new things simply for the joy of doing them—not to be the best.

Parents who encourage their kids to try new things provide an atmosphere that fosters creativity. Challenge your child to find creative solutions to his problems. Show him by example how to relax, have fun, and even how to laugh at himself. Creativity is stifled when people take themselves too seriously. Within the proper boundaries, give your kids permission to take risks. Let them fail—and remind them that most great inventors have failed at first, too!

How curious are you? If you read a word you don't recognize, do you take time to look it up? When you see something new on a walk, do you stop to investigate? Set an example of curiosity for your child.

Remind children that it's okay to make mistakes—we all do!

Discover new ways to be expressive.

Most children possess gifts and abilities that lay dormant, waiting for opportunities to emerge. One way to help children uncover these latent talents is by encouraging them to discover new ways to express themselves. You may not see it now, but there might be a great musician, artist, dancer, writer, poet, mechanic, engineer, scientist, inventor, or government leader just waiting to emerge in your child!

Who would have thought the young shepherd boy David would one day become a famous poet, mighty warrior, and powerful king? What citizen of Nazareth would have guessed the child Jesus would one day be revealed to the world as the Savior of humankind? We never know what plans God has in store for even the youngest of children. But as parents, we can give our children every opportunity to discover their niche and find new ways to be expressive.

TARGET MOMENT

As soon as your child shows interest in an instrument, sport, or hobby, help her learn more about it. It may be a passing fancy, but you may also be encouraging a lifelong pursuit!

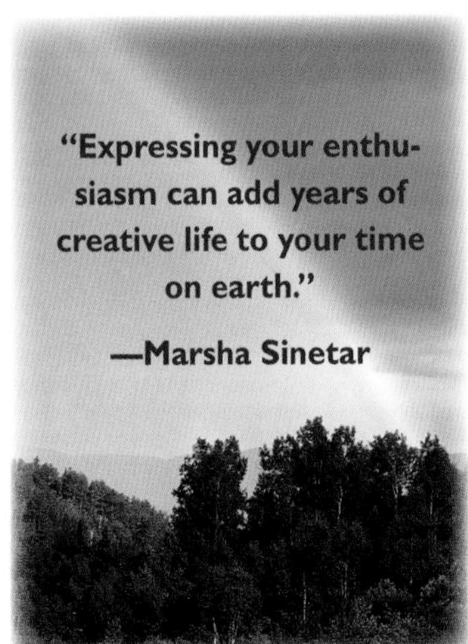

Some children naturally seek new ways to express themselves. Does your child often go to the piano to bang out an unrecognizable tune? This may be a sign of latent musical talent. Does your child spend hours with crayons, construction paper, glue, and glitter? You may have a budding artist. Encourage your child to be expressive—but do not force him to do things he doesn't enjoy.

Look for opportunities to introduce your child to new forms of expression without placing unnecessary pressure on him. Take family trips to the symphony, the opera, the zoo, museums, and parks. Do you have a hobby? Invite your child to share it with you. If you have the slightest inclination that your child may be developing an interest in an activity, find a way to introduce him to it. Then let his natural curiosity and creativity take over!

TRY THIS!

Check out books and videos that deal with an area of interest to your child. Do you have a local chamber of commerce or visitor's bureau? Contact organizations for activities and cultural events.

Intelligence is measured in many ways.

As we encourage our children to use their minds to love and serve God, we must remember that intelligence can be measured in many ways. Since its inception in the early 1900s, the traditional intelligence quotient (IQ) test has come under criticism. Critics insist such tests are invariably skewed, since questions cannot be equally meaningful for members of different sociocultural groups. Add to this the fact that people solve problems in different ways, and you can see how inaccurate such tests can be.

What really makes a person smart? Some are "book smart," while others are "street smart." Some have accumulated facts, while others possess common sense. The bottom line is that measured intelligence doesn't determine a person's success. According to Thomas J. Stanley in *The Millionaire Mind* (Andrews McMeel Publishing, 2000), the average millionaire today maintained less than a 3.0 GPA in school. For these individuals, drive—not test scores—determined success.

There are many ways to measure intelligence, including …

wisdom

love

creativity

compassion

talents

key point

THERE ARE MANY WAYS TO BE SMART.

This means your child has great potential regardless of her school grades. It means she can love and serve God with all her mind, even if her mind is not perfect. Children with learning disabilities or mental impairments can love and honor God as effectively as the most brilliant child! And if a mind is completely incapable of knowing or loving or honoring God, be assured God understands that, too, and He will respond to that mind with love, mercy, and grace.

Wisdom is another form of intelligence. Where knowledge is the collection of information, wisdom is the application of knowledge. Parents who want their children to love God with all their minds will encourage them to seek God and His Word—and to acquire wisdom that results in love, obedience, and reverence for God. Wisdom that is "first of all pure; then peace-loving, considerate, submissive, full of mercy and good fruit, impartial and sincere" (James 3:17).

TIPS FOR TODDLERS

Read, read, read! Many parents begin reading to their children before they're born and continue the practice throughout their early years of development. Read to your toddlers each day!

Check out these online resources for parents of children with disabilities.

- **American Association of People with Disabilities (www.aapd.com)**
- **Attention Deficit Disorder Association (www.add.org)**
- **American Foundation for the Blind (www.afb.org)**
- **Council for Exceptional Children (www.cec.sped.org)**
- **American Association on Mental Retardation (www.aamr.org)**
- **International Dyslexia Organization (www.interdys.org)**
- **National Center for Learning Disabilities (www.ncld.org)**

With All Your Strength

Loving God with all your strength is the key to physical fitness. Maintaining a strong and healthy body demonstrates stewardship and encourages service. It demonstrates stewardship because we are nurturing and caring for the bodies God has given us. It encourages service because it makes us fit and ready to do whatever God calls us to do.

Physical fitness is more than muscles.

When we hear the words "physical fitness," we often picture sleek athletes or imposing bodybuilders. But there is more to being physically fit than playing sports and lifting weights. Those pursuits are fine for some, but they aren't for everyone. The real essence of physical fitness is developing and maintaining good health.

Being fit means being ready.

Semper Paratus is the motto of the United States Coast Guard. The Latin phrase means "always ready." The Coast Guard stands ready to protect, defend, and secure us at a moment's notice. When it comes to physical fitness, *Semper Paratus* could be the Christian's motto, too. By maintaining good health we stay focused, alert, and ready to tackle life's challenges—and God's will.

The motto of the Coast Guard is *Semper Paratus*, or "always ready." Are you ready to serve with all your strength?

A recent report from the Surgeon General titled "Physical Health and Activity" revealed surprising results!

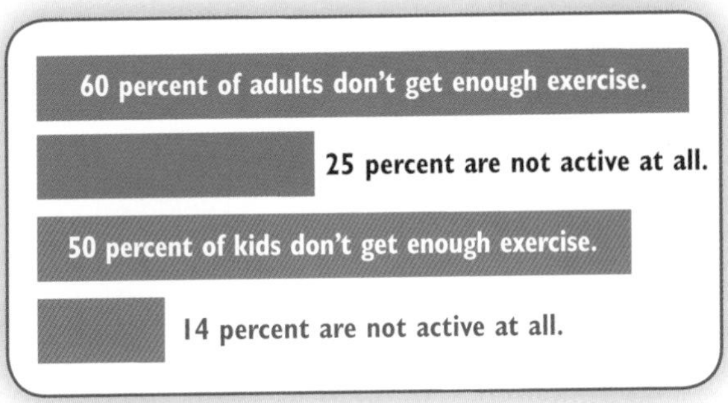

- 60 percent of adults don't get enough exercise.
- 25 percent are not active at all.
- 50 percent of kids don't get enough exercise.
- 14 percent are not active at all.

Keeping physically fit helps us serve God. A lack of physical fitness can lead to disease, sickness, and even death. According to the American Heart Association, even moderate physical activity reduces heart disease, high blood pressure, obesity, and diabetes. God doesn't want us to worship our bodies, but He does want us to be ready and willing to serve Him.

key point
STAY PHYSICALLY ACTIVE.

key point
FITNESS AIDS PREPAREDNESS.

Regular exercise helps us ...

- **Improve heart health.**
- **Increase muscle strength.**
- **Strengthen the immune system.**
- **Maintain or lose weight.**
- **Prevent diseases.**
- **Boost self-esteem.**

Even though research shows the benefits of physical activity, many adults in America do not get enough physical activity to provide health benefits. Inactivity increases with age and is more common among women than men. Many children aren't physically active enough to promote long-term health benefits! And like adults, adolescent activity declines with age—female teens being less physically active than their male counterparts.

Being fit improves our quality of life.

Children who are active and physically fit often enjoy a greater sense of well-being. Other benefits include an improved ability to handle stress, reduced risk of physical injury, weight control, and healthful sleep patterns. Kids who learn to value physical fitness are more likely to remain physically fit as adults.

When God placed Adam and Eve in the garden, the couple enjoyed perfect health. We'll enjoy perfect health in Heaven, too. It's different today, though. Perfect health is not guaranteed. But that doesn't mean God isn't concerned about our physical health. In fact, we honor God by taking good care of the bodies He has given us and the health He blesses us with—and staying healthy helps us serve God as well.

TIPS FOR 'TWEENS

When your child reaches his 'tweens, fitness and appearance become much more important. Let your child know you love him for who he is—not for how he looks. Encourage fitness, but focus on the inner person.

Read 1 Corinthians 6:19, 20 with your child. Consider the following questions together:

- *Why is the word "temple" used to describe our bodies as a dwelling place for God's Spirit?*
- *What price was paid to purchase us?*
- *How can you honor God with your body?*

The apostle Paul viewed caring for our physical bodies as an act of stewardship and worship. "Do you not know that your body is a temple of the Holy Spirit, who is in you, whom you have received from God?" (1 Corinthians 6:19, 20). Help your child realize the importance of honoring God with health and fitness!

Set a healthy example for your kids by engaging in regular physical exercise—or better yet, exercise with your kids!

- *Challenge the cultural mindset.* Some experts look to body fat as an indicator of health, but the danger lies in thinking all people are built alike. Some simply carry more body fat; and a little body fat is actually a healthy thing.
- *Change your perspective.* Don't buy the marketing ploy that says thinner is better—this has driven some kids to eating disorders.
- *Choose your path.* Don't emphasize body image; emphasize body *health*. Set a course that focuses on exercise and proper nutrition rather than appearance.

- **How does being fit express the quality of your life?**
- **Can your child see that fitness is important to you?**
- **Is health a part of your daily routine?**
- **What healthy changes can you make?**

Eating right helps us be fit.

One of the amazing things about the human body is the way God designed it to be nourished and fueled by the good things He placed on earth for us to eat. A balanced diet helps build strong bodies, prevents disease, and contributes to a general sense of well-being.

God provides food for fitness.

God said to Adam and Eve, "I give you every seed-bearing plant on the face of the whole earth and every tree that has fruit with seed in it. They will be yours for food" (Genesis 1:29). Many nutritionists talk about eating "close to the earth," or eating natural foods from the plants and animals God created for us. Some studies show a balanced diet from natural foods may eliminate the need for vitamin and mineral supplements.

Daniel was likely a teenager when he was deported to Babylon. Alone in a foreign country, Daniel faced a difficult dilemma. Would he eat the rich, royal food offered or stand for God and refuse to eat such defiled food? He chose to follow God and ate only vegetables and water. The result? Daniel looked healthier than the young men who ate the rich food. The benefits of good food should not be overlooked.

Eating an adequate number of servings daily from each food group provides necessary nutrients to maintain good health without contributing to weight gain or loss.

Ideally we'd all eat the right foods so we wouldn't require nutritional supplements. But since we often don't, provide a daily vitamin and mineral supplement. This ensures your child is receiving the nutrients he needs.

The United States Department of Agriculture recently updated its popular food-guide pyramid. The new recommendations for daily consumption are:

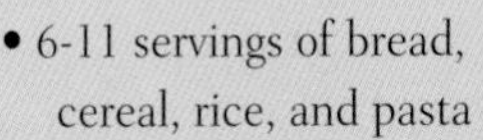

- 6-11 servings of bread, cereal, rice, and pasta
- 3-5 servings of vegetables
- 2-4 servings of fruit
- 2-3 servings of milk, yogurt, and cheese
- 2-3 servings of meat, poultry, fish, dry beans, eggs, and nuts
- sparing use of fats, oils, and sweets

Here are a few tips for parents who want to promote healthy eating habits in their kids. Make sure your child eats breakfast. Provide a wide variety of foods. Reduce fats used in cooking. Limit sugar. Serve water or milk in place of sweetened fruit drinks or colas. Let kids help plan and prepare meals. Finally, set a healthy example for your children in the way you eat.

When it comes to diet and nutrition, what kind of example are you setting for your child? What do you think your child learns from the way you eat at home, at restaurants, or at church dinners?

What we eat affects how we feel.

A recent government study showed that deaths due to poor diet and physical inactivity rose by 33 percent over the past decade and may soon overtake tobacco as the leading preventable cause of death in the United States. But our diet affects more than our physical health. Refined sugars are often labeled "empty calories" because they provide calories to the body without nutritional benefit. Our body responds by depleting itself of its own supply of nutrients to process these empty calories.

The term "sugar blues" is a type of melancholy caused by excessive consumption of sugary foods.

Prepared, processed, sugar-laden, and "fast" foods are readily available to today's consumer. But a constant diet of such nonnutritional foods damages our bodies. Fatigue is a common symptom of a poor diet. Other symptoms include irritability, lack of concentration, depression, and an inability to concentrate. On the other hand, a healthful diet increases energy levels, enhances concentration, and lifts spirits. For many people, just knowing they're taking care of their bodies makes them feel more confident.

Sometimes parents inadvertently encourage sugar consumption in young children. Here are a few things to avoid:

- *Don't send a young child to bed with juice in a bottle.*
- *Don't feed kids sugary foods to keep them quiet or occupied.*
- *Make desserts after meals the exception, not the rule.*

One key to avoiding the junk-food trap is learning to plan ahead. Plan your meals and do your grocery shopping according to your plan. When we're busy, we may be tempted to feed our families with the most convenient foods. Often, though, what is the most convenient isn't the healthiest, and we end up compromising our nutritional needs for the sake of time and simplicity. Fast foods with empty calories may leave kids barely able to keep their heads off their desks or the energy to get up off the couch.

The average American eats the equivalent of 20 teaspoons of sugar a day. (U.S. FDA)

Children are powerfully affected by what they eat. A study in *Lancet* reported that 79 percent of hyperactive children in a test group improved when sugar-laden foods and foods with artificial colorings and flavorings were restricted in their diets. When the foods were reintroduced, behaviors worsened. Perhaps the most helpful thing parents can do is to eliminate much of the sugary foods their kids eat. Allow them as special treats, but don't make them commonplace in your home.

TARGET MOMENT

Help kids make the connection between how they feel or act and what they eat. When your child becomes too active after eating sugary foods, explain the connection between food and how we feel. Explain why you limit sugar.

Exercise good choices when selecting food.

When given the option, most children will not choose a healthful, balanced diet. Fast foods and sugary snacks are too tempting! But by eliminating unhealthy choices, you will help your kids in many ways—immediately by giving them good food to stay healthy, and in the long run by teaching them good food choices.Make sure you set the right example in your own eating and snacking habits!

According to most nutritionists, the largest portion of daily food should be whole-grain breads, cereals, and other starches. These foods provide energy, fiber, and essential minerals. Another important rule is to use brown rice and whole-grain breads in place of white rice, bread, and pasta. Provide a wide color variety of fruits and vegetables. Dairy products promote good bone health. Choose low fat varieties. Finally, eat protein to provide the amino acids our bodies require.

Remember: you are what you eat! Encourage your child to make healthy food choices.

On a piece of paper, create a chart based on the USDA revised food pyramid. Use the chart as a framework for your shopping list. Take your child with you to help choose foods from the categories on your list.

Invite your child to go along when you shop for groceries. Choose fresh fruits and vegetables; read labels to avoid excess sodium and preservatives; select fresh meat, fish, and poultry; and choose natural ingredients. Let your kids join you in the kitchen, too. Tell them why you choose to bake and roast meats rather than fry them and why you choose to steam vegetables rather than cover them in rich sauces. Let your kids

School lunches can teach kids to make wise food choices. Many kids choose cafeteria foods to eat—and not always with good nutrition in mind. Why not pack a lunch? Keep healthful lunch items on hand and encourage your child to choose from the food-guide pyramid. When it comes to snack time, keep nuts, cheese, peanut butter, and fresh fruit on hand instead of chips or cookies. Remind your child that healthy choices keep us full of energy and ready for whatever comes our way!

TIPS FOR 'TWEENS

Most 'tweens love to snack, so maintain special snack shelves in your refrigerator and kitchen cabinet stocked with healthy foods to eat between meals.

Physically fit people have energy, handle stress better, sleep soundly, and tend to have a positive outlook on life.

Kids-Can-Make-It Recipes

LUNCH BOX WRAPS

1 package flour tortillas
sliced ham or turkey
sliced cheese
shredded lettuce
your child's favorite salad dressing

- Pour salad dressing on tortilla.
- Place meat, cheese, and lettuce on tortilla.
- Roll and eat.

PUMPKIN SMOOTHIES

1/8 teaspoon nutmeg
1/2 cup canned pumpkin
3/4 cup milk or vanilla yogurt
1/4 teaspoon cinnamon
2 teaspoons brown sugar
4 ice cubes

- Combine all ingredients in a blender and puree until smooth.
- Pour the smoothies into small glasses.

(For a fun touch, add colored candy sprinkles!)

TROPICAL MIX

I cup dried banana chips

I cup flaked coconut

I cup chocolate chips

3 cups oat or corn cereal

- Mix all ingredients in a gallon-sized plastic bag.
- Shake well.
- Nibble and enjoy!

FISH IN A POND

I/4 cup softened, low-fat cream cheese

fish-shaped crackers

4 celery stalks

- Scoop cream cheese into a bowl.
- Place crackers in a separate bowl.
- Dip celery sticks into cheese, then into bowl to "catch" a fish.

CHICKEN SALAD CONES

I can white-meat chicken

4 ice-cream cones

I/2 cup mayonnaise

2 teaspoons pickle relish

- Open canned chicken and drain.
- Put chicken into bowl, add mayonnaise.
- Add relish and stir.
- Fill cones with scoops of chicken salad.

Kids-Can-Make-It Recipes

PEANUT BUTTER BALLS

2/3 cup crushed corn flakes
2/3 cup shredded coconut
1/3 cup smooth peanut butter
2 tablespoons honey

- Mix the ingredients well using half of the cornflakes.
- Shape into small balls.
- Roll balls in the remaining corn flakes.

(These cookies can be put in the fridge to firm up. They also freeze well.)

FROZEN FRUIT CUP

1 cup apple sauce
1 10-ounce package frozen strawberries, thawed
1 can mandarin oranges, drained
2 tablespoons orange juice (or other fruit juice)
1 cup grapes
paper cups (plastic may crack)

- Combine all ingredients in a bowl.
- Mix and pour into paper cups.
- Freeze overnight.

"SIMPLY FRUIT" SALAD

1 cup blueberries
1 package frozen strawberries
1 orange, peeled and sectioned
1 can sliced peaches, drained
1 cup seedless grapes

- Thaw and drain the strawberries.
- Wash the fruit and combine in large bowl.
- Serve in paper cups.

BANANA WRAPS

1 8-inch flour tortilla
2 tablespoons peanut butter
2 tablespoons fruit spread
1 small banana, peeled

- Place tortilla on a paper towel. Microwave for 10 seconds (until the tortilla is soft and warm).
- Spread with peanut butter, then top with fruit spread.
- Place the banana to one edge of the tortilla. Fold up the bottom of tortilla. Bring the edge over the banana and roll it up.

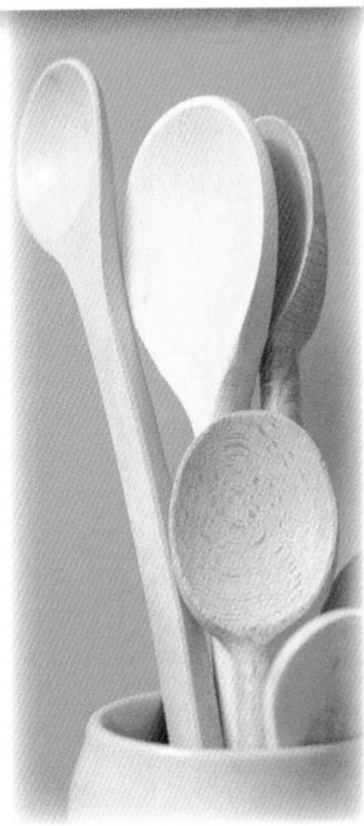

Kids-Can-Make-It Recipes

YOGURT POPS

2 cups plain yogurt

1/3 cup frozen orange juice concentrate

1 tablespoon honey

- Combine ingredients in bowl. Mix well.
- Pour into paper cups and freeze for an hour.
- Insert a stick into the center of each pop and return to the freezer until frozen.
- To serve, hold a warm hand around the cup for a minute, then push the bottom to release the yogurt pop.

FRUIT SOUP

honeydew and/or cantaloupe

1 banana

grapes

1 cup frozen orange juice

1 scoop frozen yogurt or sorbet

- Scoop balls from melons with a melon-ball cutter.
- Slice a banana with a plastic knife.
- Place fruit in a bowl.
- Add the orange juice.
- Pour the fruit soup over scoops of frozen yogurt or sorbet.

PEANUT BUTTER & CHOCOLATE CHIP TORTILLA

1 8-inch flour tortilla

peanut butter

mini chocolate chips

- Spread a thin layer of peanut butter on an open tortilla.
- Sprinkle chocolate chips on the peanut butter.
- Roll up the tortilla and enjoy!

ASTRONAUT PUDDING

1 small box instant pudding mix

1 cup milk

self-locking sandwich bags

plastic drinking straws

- Place 2 tablespoons of instant pudding in a self-locking bag.
- Add 1/4 cup milk.
- Seal the bag and squish the pudding mix gently.
- Open the bag a bit and slide in a drinking straw.

(You can eat just like the astronauts—with no utensils!)

Exercise helps us be fit.

There is a grain of truth in the old adage, "No pain, no gain." Physical exercise provides many benefits to our bodies, but not without some effort on our part. It isn't always easy or convenient, but the benefits we derive from exercise are worth the effort!

Exercise strengthens both bodies and minds.

Exercise can be grouped into two categories. *Aerobic exercises* utilize large muscles such as the heart and lungs to strengthen the heart and enhance the lungs' ability to distribute oxygen efficiently throughout the body.

Aerobic exercises include running, bicycling, swimming, in-line skating, cross-country skiing, aerobic dance, fitness walking, and jumping rope. Most experts recommend 30-60 minutes of sustained aerobic exercise three to five times a week.

"Physical fitness is not only one of the most important keys to a healthy body, it is the basis of dynamic and creative intellectual activity."
—John F. Kennedy

Anaerobic exercises work muscles intensely for short periods of time. Anaerobic activities cannot be sustained for long periods because they do not use oxygen for energy and produce lactic acid, which must be burned up. Anaerobic exercises include weight lifting and sprinting. Strength training increases the body's metabolic rate, which burns more calories. It increases bone density and lean muscle mass. Both aerobic and anaerobic exercises are necessary to achieve optimal fitness.

TARGET MOMENT

The Center for Mental Health Services (1998) indicates that as many as one in 33 children and one in eight teens may have depression. Talk with your child about depression and point to exercise as one possible treatment.

PARENTS POINTER

If your child is overweight or lacks coordination, choose activities he can enjoy—without embarrassment. Go on walks, ride bicycles, or take a hike. Creatively insert exercise into his daily routine without making him feel self-conscious.

Regular exercise provides intellectual, psychological, and emotional benefits as well. Studies show that exercise can sharpen mental abilities, improve mathematical functions, and even improve creativity. This is partly because exercise elevates brain chemicals such as endorphins and serotonin—natural pain medication and chemicals that help us feel happier. Each of these chemicals is released naturally in the body as a result of vigorous physical activity.

The American Heart Association recommends that children ages two and older get at least 30 minutes of moderate activity every day and 30 minutes of vigorous activity several times a week. Commit to a regular exercise schedule. Walk to the store instead of driving. Rake the yard or walk the dog.

Brain chemicals released by exercise	What those chemicals do for us
ENDORPHINS	Natural pain medication, three times more potent than morphine
DOPAMINE	Affects emotional responses and ability to experience pleasure
SEROTONIN	Creates general happiness, calms anxiety, relieves depression

Choose exercises you can stick with.

One of the great things about physical exercise is that we have such a wide variety of activities from which to choose. Don't settle for workouts you find boring. Choose exercises or a range of exercises you can stick with. Try a new sport or physical activity. Work out with a partner. Play background music or exercise outdoors near forests, parks, lakes, and beaches. Doing what you enjoy in a pleasant environment will help you sustain your commitment.

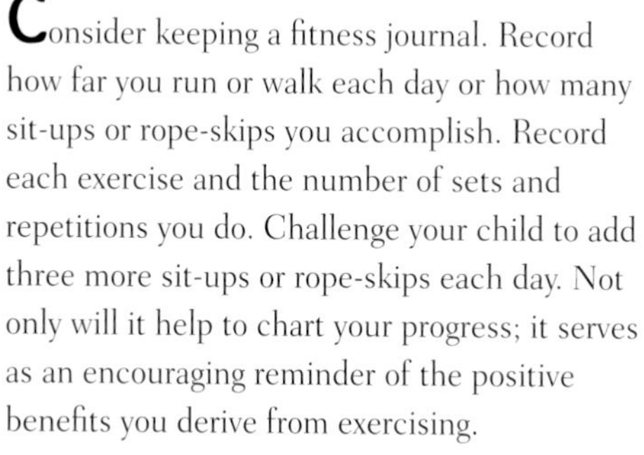

Consider keeping a fitness journal. Record how far you run or walk each day or how many sit-ups or rope-skips you accomplish. Record each exercise and the number of sets and repetitions you do. Challenge your child to add three more sit-ups or rope-skips each day. Not only will it help to chart your progress; it serves as an encouraging reminder of the positive benefits you derive from exercising.

MAKE A SIMPLE CHART TO HELP YOU AND YOUR CHILD STICK WITH YOUR FITNESS PLANS!

DATE:

WHAT I DID TODAY:

HOW I FELT:

MY PLAN FOR TOMORROW:

Setting goals is an important part of your exercise routine. A long-range goal may be to lose weight or to improve your endurance, stamina, and energy level. Short-range goals might include attending a fitness class each week or taking a daily walk. Setting and working toward goals is an important skill for kids—and ones that carry over to other areas of their lives. Plus, kids feel good knowing they've reached a goal they set for themselves!

The Special Olympics offers training and competition to more than a million people with disabilities in over 150 countries. See www.specialolympics.org to locate the nearest venue.

Kids' goals may include making a sports team or beating their personal best in the mile run. Others may include weight loss or simply engaging in some physical activity a certain number of days per week in the goals they set. Help your child write out inspirational quotations from athletes, coaches, and others to keep around the house. Encourage your child to reach his goals, but remember that fitness is only one aspect of our lives and should be kept in balance.

key point

DON'T BECOME OBSESSED!

TIPS FOR 'TWEENS

Be sensitive to your 'tween's self-esteem when setting fitness goals. Emphasize exercise, but don't dwell on weight, body image, and so on. Stress the benefits of exercise!

It's difficult to sustain activities we don't enjoy. Choose workouts and activities you can stick with!

Turn workouts into family fun.

Parents who want to encourage their kids to stay physically fit must find ways to make fitness fun for the whole family. When your kids are young, make sure to purchase a number of "active" toys for them—toys that require wagons, plastic slides, tyke bikes, jump ropes, and balls. As kids get older, try kick balls, soccer balls, or even a ping-pong table. Guide them (don't force them) into organized sports. Encourage them to be competitive without placing undue emphasis on winning.

There are many ways to encourage a love of physical activity in children without making them feel they're being forced into it. Designate one night each week "Family Fitness Night." Take turns choosing the activities each time. You might find yourselves playing basketball or rollerblading in the park. You might even graduate to nine holes of golf or a trip to the rock-climbing center!

key point

DO FAMILY FITNESS.

"Everybody needs beauty as well as bread, places to play in and pray in, where nature may heal and give strength to body and soul."

—John Muir

Parents, stay in the best physical shape possible so you can stay active with your kids. Don't just set the rules—set the example!

10,000 steps = five miles!

Family fitness doesn't have to be strenuous. The 10,000 Step Challenge encourages people of all ages to take 10,000 steps every day. With a simple step counter, or pedometer (available in most sporting-goods stores), you and your family can keep track of the number of steps you take daily. The key is to wear your pedometer all day and to find ways to steadily increase your number of steps each day.

Purchase inexpensive pedometers for everyone, and encourage your family to take the 10,000 Step Challenge.

TIPS FOR TODDLERS

Consider these guides for physical activity for toddlers.

- **Toddlers should accumulate 30 minutes daily of structured physical activity.**
- **Toddlers should develop large-motor skills.**
- **Toddlers need indoor and outdoor areas for performing large-muscle activities.**

Above all, make family fitness fun. If you have small children, turn a simple walk into a scavenger hunt and give kids a list of special objects to find. Make a rule during croquet that, after each hit, you must run to the ball. Consider enrolling your entire family in the President's Challenge program (www.presidentschallenge.org). The program includes fitness goals for every family member and every age group from children to senior adults. You can even work together to earn the Presidential Active Lifestyle Award!

STRENGTH-TRAINING LOG

Name: **Start Date:**

EXERCISE	DATE:					
	lbs.					
	reps.					
	lbs.					
	reps.					
	lbs.					
	reps.					
	lbs.					
	reps.					
	lbs.					
	reps.					
	lbs.					
	reps.					
	lbs.					
	reps.					
	lbs.					
	reps.					
	lbs.					
	reps.					
	lbs.					
	reps.					
	lbs.					
	reps.					
	lbs.					
	reps.					
	lbs.					
	reps.					
	lbs.					
	reps.					
	lbs.					
	reps.					
	lbs.					
	reps.					

WALKING LOG

Name: Start Date:

ROUTE	DATE						
	distance						
	time						
	distance						
	time						
	distance						
	time						
	distance						
	time						
	distance						
	time						
	distance						
	time						
	distance						
	time						
	distance						
	time						
	distance						
	time						
	distance						
	time						
	distance						
	time						
	distance						
	time						
	distance						
	time						
	distance						
	time						
	distance						
	time						
	distance						
	time						

Cleanliness helps us be fit.

Diet and exercise are vital to a child's physical health, but they aren't the only factors. Cleanliness is another important element of good health. As we teach our children personal hygiene and protecting themselves from bacteria, we're adding to their physical health.

Clean bodies improve our outlook on life.

Some say the phrase "Cleanliness is next to godliness" is an old Hebrew proverb. If that's true, it wouldn't be surprising. God gave the ancient Hebrews specific guidelines about sanitation, contact with dead bodies, and cleansing from infectious skin diseases and other forms of uncleanness. Often the instructions involved washing with water. Thousands of years later, modern science has confirmed the hygienic principles God taught ancient Israel.

The prescription for preventing the spread of diseases and everyday "bugs" is good hygiene!

"SOAP AND WATER AND COMMON SENSE ARE THE BEST DISINFECTANTS."

—WILLIAM OSLER

In the early years, parents are responsible for their children's personal hygiene. They change diapers, give baths, wipe noses, and wash hands. In time parents move from doers to teachers, helping their children develop good hygiene, including that hygiene prevents the spread of disease. This is especially important for school-age children, since many of the illnesses they'll be exposed to will come from school and other social environments.

Hand washing is one of the first hygienic principles kids can learn. In addition to hand washing, teach your children the importance of daily bathing. Many kids dislike baths or showers simply because it interrupts playtime. Teach them the importance of keeping their whole bodies clean. Explain that hair washing and brushing are important, as is trimming fingernails and toenails. As they reach puberty, introduce your kids to deodorants and grooming products.

Kids need to learn that personal grooming makes us nicer to be around!

Since we can't see bacteria, it's hard for many children to understand the importance of washing their hands. Ask your child to demonstrate how she washes. Then coat her hands with a mixture of 1/8 teaspoon of cinnamon and 1/8 cup vegetable oil and wash again. There will be cinnamon remaining after washing. Encourage her to keep washing until all the cinnamon is gone. Explain that this is how long she must wash her hands to get rid of harmful bacteria every day!

Bath or shower time may seem like drudgery to some kids, so here's a way to make it memorable. The next time it rains hard (no lightning!), let your child go outside in her swimsuit with a bar of soap and take a "shower" outdoors. It will give you both something fun to remember!

Clean teeth invite others to smile.

Dental hygiene is more than having a pleasant smile. It's another important contributor to health and fitness. Some studies have linked tooth and gum health to overall health. Gum disease has been connected to medical conditions like stroke, diabetes, heart attack, and even lung disease. Bacteria sent through the bloodstream causes plaque build-up in arteries and affects the way we control blood sugars. Parents are wise to help their kids develop habits of good dental hygiene.

Kids' dental care should begin when their first teeth appear. As children grow, they should take on the responsibility of brushing their teeth morning and evening, establishing a regular pattern of brushing. Teach your kids to brush gently, holding the brush at a 45-degree angle to the gum line, then cleaning the chewing surfaces and outside and inside surfaces with sweeping strokes. Finally, gently brush the tongue and the roof of the mouth.

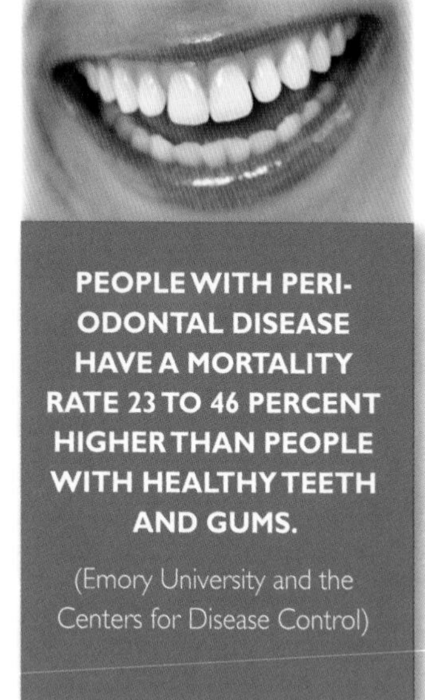

PEOPLE WITH PERIODONTAL DISEASE HAVE A MORTALITY RATE 23 TO 46 PERCENT HIGHER THAN PEOPLE WITH HEALTHY TEETH AND GUMS.

(Emory University and the Centers for Disease Control)

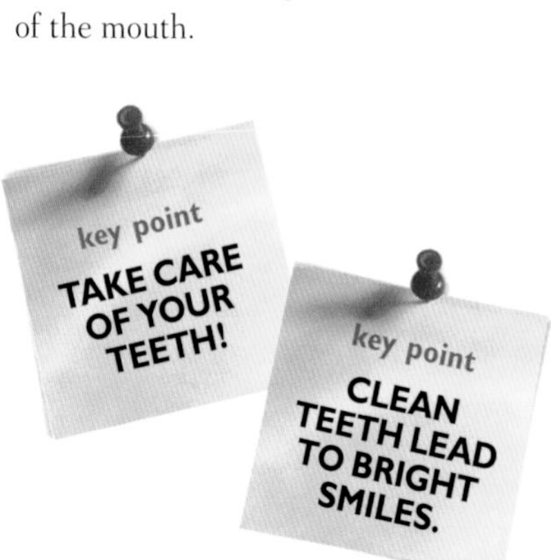

"Every time you smile at someone, it is an action of love, a gift to that person, a beautiful thing."

—Mother Teresa

Brushing alone won't remove all food particles and plaque, so you'll need to teach your children to floss. When using mouthwash, choose an antiseptic variety that kills germs to reduce plaque build-up. Look for the seal of the American Dental Association on the label. In addition to reducing cavities, good oral hygiene often prevents bad breath, or halitosis. Get your kids to the dentist for regular checkups, too.

If a child is old enough to write his name, he is old enough to clean his teeth alone.

Guidelines to consider when selecting a toothbrush:

- Ask your dentist to suggest a brush that works well.
- Choose a toothbrush with soft bristles.
- Choose a small brush for children.
- Replace toothbrushes every three to four months.

Help your kids make the connection between food choices and dental health. Sugary foods and carbonated drinks expose the mouth to acids that harm the teeth's protective enamel. We should remind our children of the benefits of having clean teeth and a bright smile. Our teeth and smile are among the first things people notice about us. If we feel confident in our smile, we often convey that confidence to others. Our smiles invites others to smile, too.

Establishing healthy habits is important.

Most sources say it takes from twenty-one to forty days to develop a habit—not much time when we have a lifetime of health to plan for! Helping our kids establish healthy habits can have a profound and long-range effect on the quality of their lives as adults.

Being healthy is a choice we make each day.

We make choices every day that affect our health. We choose the amount of sleep and food we have. We choose our level of physical activity. It's the same with kids. For a time, we choose for them. We set their bedtimes, buy and prepare the food they eat, and choose family activities. But we can't always make these decisions for them. That's why it's important to teach them at an early age to make wise decisions about their health.

What kind of choices can we teach our kids to make? We can teach them to eat for health. We can teach them the value of regular exercise and the importance of a good night's sleep. We can teach them to value cleanliness, knowing that they're preventing illnesses and disease when they do. We can walk them through their disappointments and use those times to teach them how to manage conflict and handle stress.

Alcohol is responsible for nearly half of all teen auto crashes!

In addition to making choices that promote good health, we must teach our kids to resist choices that result in poor health. We must teach them about the dangers of tobacco—that smoking is the main cause of heart and lung disease. We must teach our children to avoid alcohol—that alcohol is harmful to the body and is the leading cause of death among teenagers. Talk to your children about the harmful affects these risky behaviors have on our bodies.

TIPS FOR 'TWEENS

Sadly, many 'tweens are caught up in substance abuse today. Discuss this problem with your child by asking, "Why would anyone intentionally do something to harm her body?" and "Why would anyone wish to not be in control of his actions?"

TARGET MOMENT

Consider your own habits as you think about these questions:

- **What good health choices do you make?**
- **What poor behaviors should you change?**
- **What do your habits say to your kids?**

Above all, we must teach our children that they honor God by making healthy choices. When we grasp the magnificence of the human mind and soul, we begin to realize how much treasure God has deposited in our physical bodies. They deserve all the care we can give them!

CELEBRATE GOOD HEALTH!

Being healthy helps us serve God.

Being healthy allows us to serve God with all our strength. God deserves our best, and that includes our physical service. And here's the beauty of His plan. We can love God with all our strength, and our strength will never be exhausted. He promises to give us more: "Those who hope in the LORD will renew their strength" (Isaiah 40:31).

Let's think about health and fitness as an investment—an investment in the growth of God's kingdom. Each day of our lives is a twenty-four-hour window of opportunity to advance God's kingdom on earth. The psalmist observed, "The length of our days is seventy years—or eighty, if we have the strength" (Psalm 90:10). None of us knows how much time we have on this earth, and many things can happen to us that are beyond our control. But where we have control, we must make sure we are fit, alert, and prepared daily to serve God and extend His kingdom. We want to instill this in our children, too, so that as we're teaching them about fitness we're also preparing them to serve God throughout their lives.

BEING FIT LETS US LEND A HAND FOR GOD—AND OTHERS!

"HE GIVES STRENGTH TO THE WEARY AND INCREASES THE POWER OF THE WEAK.... THEY WILL SOAR ON WINGS LIKE EAGLES." (ISAIAH 40:29, 31)

When asked which of God's commandments is greatest, Jesus said: "Love the Lord your God with all your heart and with all your soul and with all your mind and with all your strength" (Mark 12:30). We serve God when we are fit emotionally, spiritually, intellectually, and physically. And it's our duty to teach and model these characteristics to our children.

"When wealth is lost, nothing is lost; when health is lost, something is lost; when character is lost, all is lost."
—Billy Graham

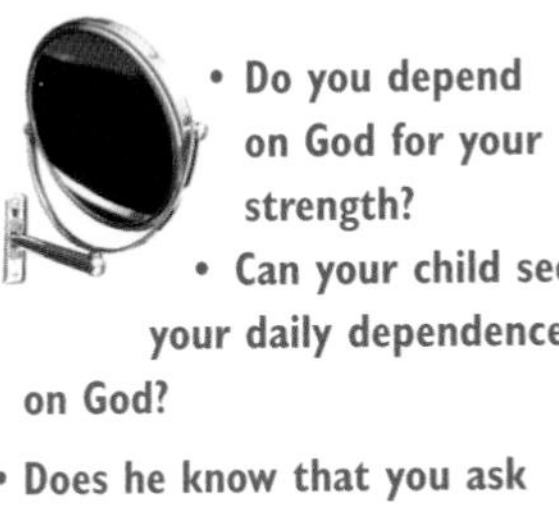

- **Do you depend on God for your strength?**
- **Can your child see your daily dependence on God?**
- **Does he know that you ask God for the strength you need?**

Remember, we lead by example!

Let's show our children how to love God with all their hearts and souls by devotion, prayer, and worship. Let's show them how to love God with all their minds by being students of the Word. Let's show them how to love God with all their strength by serving God and His church through their time, talents, and resources.

LET'S TEACH OUR KIDS THE TRUE MEANING OF FITNESS!

More Resources

BOOKS

- John MacArthur, *What The Bible Says About Parenting: Biblical Principles for Raising Godly Children* (W Publishing Group, 2000).
- William Sears et al., *The Complete Book of Christian Parenting and Child Care: A Medical and Moral Guide to Raising Happy, Healthy Children* (Broadman & Holman, 1997).
- Walt Larimore, *God's Design for the Highly Healthy Child* (Zondervan, 2005).
- Sharon Broer, *Train Up Your Children in the Ways They Should Eat* (Charisma House, 1999).
- Jayne Ray Garrison, *Living With a Challenging Child: Encouragement for Mothers of Children With ADD, Hyperactivity, or Other Behavioral Problems* (Vine Books, 1996).
- Jack Wingfield, *Growing Up Now: Your Changing Body, Your Changing Feelings* (Chariot Victor, 1991).
- Sharon Hersh, *Mom, I Feel Fat: Becoming Your Daughter's Ally in Developing a Healthy Body Image* (Shaw, 2001).

- David R. Foster et al., *Indoor Action Games for Elementary Children: Active Games and Academic Activities for Fun and Fitness* (Parker Publishing Company, 1989).

- Mary L. Gavin, *Fit Kids: A Practical Guide to Raising Active and Healthy Children From Birth to Teens* (DK Publishing, 2004).

VIDEOS AND DVDS

- ***Bringing Up Boys Parenting Videos,*** by James Dobson (Focus on the Family/Tyndale House, 2001).

- ***Little Kicks: Fitness Workout for Kids, Volume 1: 100% Pure Fun*** (Pro-Active Entertainment, 2001).

- ***Little Kicks: Fitness Workout for Kids, Volume 2: Bring It On!*** (Pro-Active Entertainment, 2004).

Subpoint Index

Chapter 3: With All Your Mind 50

Chapter 4: With All Your Strength 60

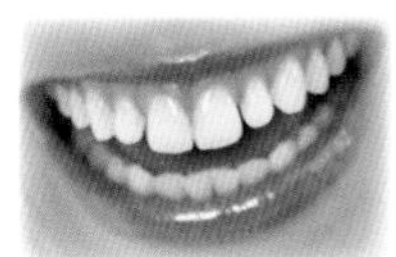